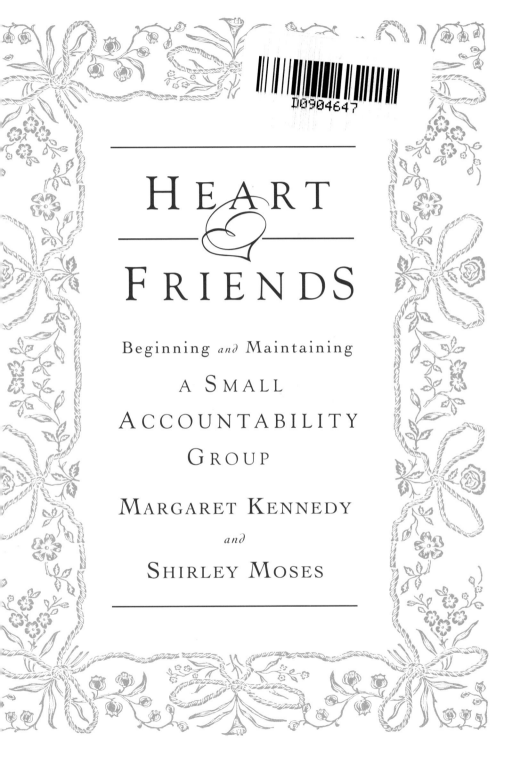

HEART

FRIENDS

Beginning *and* Maintaining

A SMALL
ACCOUNTABILITY
GROUP

MARGARET KENNEDY

and

SHIRLEY MOSES

Published by LifeWay Press®
© 2005 • Margaret Kennedy and Shirley Moses

No part of this book may be reproduced or transmitted in any form or by any means, electronic or mechanical, including photocopying and recording, or by any information storage or retrieval system, except as may be expressly permitted in writing by the publisher. Requests for permission should be addressed in writing to LifeWay Press®; One LifeWay Plaza; Nashville, TN 37234-0175.

ISBN 1-4158-2818-0

This book is CG-1126 in the Women's Enrichment category of the Christian Growth Study Plan.

Dewey Decimal Classification Number: **248.843**
Subject Heading: WOMEN \ RESPONSIBILITY \ CHRISTIAN LIFE

To order additional copies of this resource, WRITE to LifeWay Church Resources Customer Service; One LifeWay Plaza; Nashville, TN 37234-0013; FAX (615) 251-5933; PHONE (800) 458-2772;

Printed in the United States of America

Leadership and Adult Publishing
LifeWay Church Resources
One LifeWay Plaza
Nashville, TN 37234-0175

CONTENTS

ABOUT THE AUTHORS

Margaret Kennedy is founder and president of Threads of Hope Ministries, a biblical speaking and writing ministry in Dothan, Alabama (*www.margaretkennedy.org*). A graduate of Troy State University, Margaret teaches on "Kingdom Seekers," a weekly radio program.

A mother and grandmother, Margaret teaches a women's Sunday School class for Ridgecrest Baptist Church in Dothan — a setting in which *Heart Friends* was refined. As a trainer for LifeWay Christian Resources, she equips leaders in women's ministry. Margaret has written several articles for *Leading Adults*.

"In Christ I live and move and have my being. Daily He continues to weave into the tapestry of my life His precious promises and eternal truths from His Word. Sharing these riches with women everywhere is my greatest passion!"

Shirley Moses is women's ministry consultant for the Southern Baptists of Texas Convention and an advisor for the Women's Ministry Team of Hagerman Baptist Church, Sherman, Texas.

In 1995 Shirley founded Women's Ministry Connection, a networking ministry that reaches north Texas. A contributor to *Transformed Lives: Taking Women's Ministry to the Next Level* (LifeWay Press), she writes women's ministry leadership articles for the LifeWay Web site (*www.lifeway.com*). Shirley has completed her advanced Certificate of Women's Ministry at New Orleans Baptist Theological Seminary.

Her passion for equipping women led Shirley to begin Beyond the Call Ministry (*www.beyondthecallministries.org*). As a conference leader and retreat speaker, Shirley lives out her life purpose: "My heart's desire is to encourage women to discover their passion for ministry."

Heart Friends is a joint labor of love. Both women have prayed over each other's writings and thoughts. At times we have identified which writer had a particular experience so you can better identify with her teachings.

GROWING TOGETHER IN GODLINESS

Surely all of us can recall Christian leaders who have fallen, confessing to a lack of accountability in their lives. In their book *Spiritual Leadership: Moving People on to God's Agenda*, Henry and Richard Blackaby cite accountability as the primary safeguard against downfall.

Leaders make themselves accountable. Most of us can name well-known speakers and evangelists — Billy Graham, for example — who seek protection and safeguarding by intentionally making themselves accountable. They submit not because they have to, but because they want to and because they understand that accountability is their lifeline.

Individuals in the limelight are not alone in the need to be held accountable. Every believer needs the safeguard of accountability. While busyness makes deep relationships difficult, it *is* possible to enjoy friendships that keep our lives with God on track. Indeed, He created us to thrive from relationships with Heart Friends who support and encourage us in our journey of faith.

Perhaps you seek a life of purity and integrity, character development, emotional stability, or help in handling temptation. An accountability group provides a safe place to explore these areas of growth.

When *Heart Friends* was first suggested for the title, I (Margaret) confess I thought it to be a catchy phrase, a cute title, an appropriate application for this study. However, God quickly began to reveal why *He* chose this particular title.

In researching the word *heart*, some commonalities surfaced. Webster's Dictionary defines heart as "the central or innermost part" of anything. The Hebrew word, *leb*, is used figuratively to describe "the feelings, the will and even the intellect; likewise for the centre of anything."[1] In the Greek, the word *kardia* means "the seat and center of human life. The seat of the desires, feelings, affections, passions, impulses"[2] *Heart* is the deep-seated core of our innermost being.

It is no wonder, then, that Scripture admonishes us to *"Keep your heart with all diligence, ..."* (Prov. 4:23, NKJV). We must work diligently to keep our hearts safe from the deception of the Enemy and the influence of the world.

Heart Friends, who might also be called heart helpers, enable us to do just that! All of us need godly friends with whom we can freely share the deep issues of our hearts (see Heb. 10:2; John 15:14). Our desire in writing this unique workbook-journal is to share the basics of beginning and maintaining a small accountability group. By joining with other women who hold the same commitment, you can soar to new heights in your relationship with God as you grow *together* in godliness through the process of accountability.

USING *HEART FRIENDS*

Heart Friends: *Beginning and Maintaining a Small Accountability Group* is a tool that may be used to motivate women in your church or community toward Christian discipleship and spiritual growth. *Heart Friends* may be used in at least three ways:

⊛ **As a means of introducing the concept of accountability to women in your church**
Women need to learn the importance of leading an accountable life, as well as how to develop close friendships within the body of Christ. Using the four, one-hour-a-week Leader Guide sessions, Shirley introduced this biblical concept to the women in her small church. Using the same content and timetable, Margaret did the same in her large church.

During the four sessions, tears were shed and emotional walls broken down. Women began to understand the need for personal accountability and for trusted companions to walk alongside them.

⊛ **As an instructional guide for group sessions**
Our groups floundered the first year, needing a format to follow and suggestions to enhance our meetings. We began to ask ourselves *Where do we go from here?* If you are facing a similar experience, then *Heart Friends* is for you! Each account-ability group member will need a personal copy.

⊛ **As an individual study for the woman who desires a more intimate walk with the Lord or more meaningful friendships with other women**
Perhaps a long-term goal is to become part of a close-knit small group with whom you can share your heart. A personal *Heart Friends* study will move you closer to that goal, as it prepares you to become a trustworthy small-group member.

Your Heart Friends journal is divided into three sections: Getting Started (pp. 8-32), Your *Heart Friends* Toolbox (pp. 33-120), and Leader Guide suggestions (pp. 121-126).

GETTING STARTED

By highlighting the biblical principles for accountability, this important content provides the foundation for a good experience with a small group. Advantages of accountability and attributes of making oneself accountable are included. Both an action plan and suggested meeting topics can help you know how to launch a group. Questions that may come up about accountability are also addressed.

Tips that address specific needs (e.g. time management), worksheets, topical guides for discussion, and journaling pages comprise this section.

⊛ **Personal Goal Worksheet and "My Personal Testimony" (pp. 34-39)**
These exercises assist women in determining God's direction for their lives. They provide excellent "safe starter" information for getting to know your small group.
⊛ **Conversation Guides (pp. 47-80)**
Conversation Guides may be used for discussion during accountability group meetings or as personal devotionals. As they address pertinent issues facing today's women, Conversation Guides can take conversations from surface levels to greater spiritual depth.
⊛ **Asking the Hard Questions (pp. 81-82)**
As God reveals His deep work in the hearts of women within your group, women will want to be held accountable for their response to Him in this area. From a list of Hard Questions, each Heart Friend may select one that confronts an issue for her. In so doing, she is giving other group members the responsibility of asking at the next meeting how she fared with that issue.
⊛ **Journaling the Journey (pp. 87-117)**
Heart Friends can use these pages to record information shared during group meetings. Such a record is a reminder to pray for specific requests and to keep the commitments made before God and their small group.

In its simplest form, journaling is a means of pouring out the contents of your heart—getting thoughts and emotions in the open so they can be sorted and sifted. Do not allow journaling to jolt you. Sometimes I (Margaret) journal every day for weeks, and then skip some time. Keep it easy.

How I delight in rereading my history with God, so easily tracing His hand, especially during times when I was forced to simply trust His heart.
⊛ **Evaluating Health and Effectiveness (p. 119)**
Use this inventory every three months to assess how your group is functioning.
⊛ **Other helpful tips**
Tips on time management, prayer, and other areas will help foster growth in godliness. Each may be used as needed or desired.

LEADER GUIDE

This section (pp. 121-126) is for use by the women's ministry leader to introduce the principles of accountability. Procedures for four sessions, each with numbered steps, help the women's leader conduct sessions based on *Heart Friends* content.

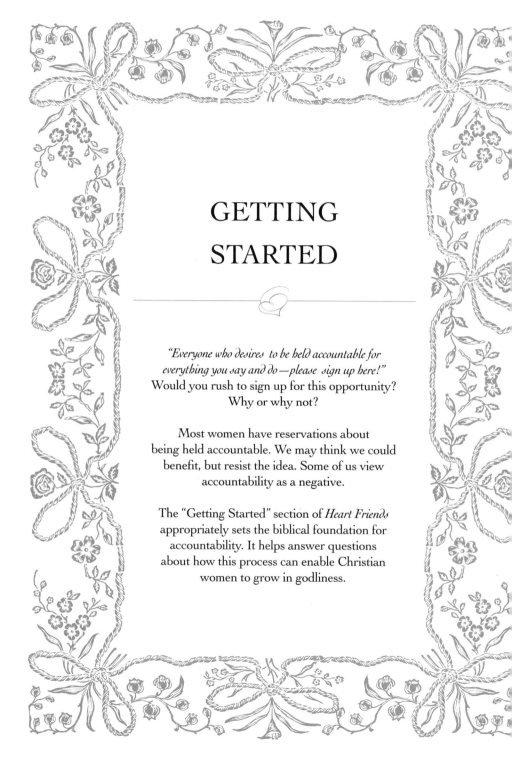

GETTING
STARTED

"Everyone who desires to be held accountable for everything you say and do—please sign up here!"
Would you rush to sign up for this opportunity?
Why or why not?

Most women have reservations about being held accountable. We may think we could benefit, but resist the idea. Some of us view accountability as a negative.

The "Getting Started" section of *Heart Friends* appropriately sets the biblical foundation for accountability. It helps answer questions about how this process can enable Christian women to grow in godliness.

ACCOUNTABILITY UNDERSTOOD

Perhaps if we understood the benefits, the security, and even the definition of accountability, we would be more eager to seek it. Let's begin by discovering what accountability means. According to Webster's Dictionary, to be *accountable* means to be "subject to having to report, explain, or justify."

How does this definition differ from your understanding? _____

_____

Read Romans 14:12.

God put the principle of accountability into place by making us accountable to Him. This accountability is inescapable and inevitable.

Our accountability to God began in the garden of Eden. In the Book of Genesis, we see how God walked daily with Adam and Eve, freely enjoying this relationship with His creation. However, after disobeying His instructions, Adam and Eve began to hide from God.

According to Genesis 3:9, God sought Adam, asking *"Where are you?"* Now why would God, who is all-seeing and all-knowing, ask such a question? It was His way of bringing man into a position of explaining why he was hiding. This verse seems to mark the first time God required His creation to explain his actions and give an account to Him.

In the same way today, God brings us to the place of continually assessing where we are with Him. Why? Because He desires to walk with His children in a relationship that is unhindered by disobedience. As God's children, we are invited to come boldy before His throne, where He promises to offer mercy and grace. First John 3:21-22 reads *"Dear friends, if our hearts do not condemn [us] we have confidence before God, and can receive whatever we ask from Him because we keep His commands and do what is pleasing in His sight."*

And 1 John 1:9 assures us that *"if we confess our sins, He is faithful and just to forgive us our sins and to cleanse us from all unrighteousness"* (NKJV). Through accountability, God keeps us in a position where He is free to reward and bless us.

Johnny Hunt, pastor of Woodstock Baptist Church, of Woodstock, Georgia, likes to say that he prays for God to "keep me clean and keep me close." Accountability requires that we welcome God to search our hearts, revealing any trace or hint of unrighteousness, so that we can stay clean and close to Him.

How does this knowledge of God's action toward you affect your understanding of the importance of accountability? _____

_____

_____

Even knowing that God first established and now requires accountability to Him does not make us naturally crave accountability. We did not inherit this desire from our first parents in the garden of Eden! Hide and Seek first took place there, when God called out to our ancestors who were attempting to hide from Him rather than confess their sin.

We are not people who run toward God. The Apostle Paul tells us that no one seeks after God (see Rom. 3:11). Left in our natural state, we are creatures who run *from* rather than *toward* taking responsibility for our actions.

Yet, knowing this about His created ones, God still calls us to accountability and—more important—He made a provision for us to experience it. He chose to come to our aid by sending His Son, Jesus, to earth and then a divine Comforter, the Holy Spirit, who takes up residence in the life of every follower of Christ. We can no longer hide from Him—nor do we need to do so!

Read John 14:16-17.

Inviting Jesus Christ to be your Savior and Lord is the first step toward living a life of accountability. The moment you make this decision, you receive your first and everlasting accountability partner—the One who can guide you into all truth and lead you wherever you need to go.

The Holy Spirit Is Your Ultimate Accountability Partner

Before we can recognize the work of the Holy Spirit, we must grasp who He is. In the upper room, Jesus taught His disciples about the Holy Spirit: *"And I will pray the Father, and He will give you another Helper, that He may abide with you forever—the Spirit of truth, whom the world cannot receive, because it neither sees Him nor knows Him; but you know Him, for He dwells with you and will be in you"* (John 14:16-17, NKJV). The Greek word used here for another, *allos*, means "another of the same kind."[3] The Holy Spirit, then, could be described as "another Jesus."

The King James Version describes the Holy Spirit as "another Comforter" (John 14:16). The Greek word for comforter is *parakletos*, which means "advocate, one who comes forward in behalf of and as the representative of another."[4] The Holy Spirit is called a Paraclete because He undertakes Christ's work in the world as He walks alongside believers acting as Christ's representatives on earth.

Jesus continued His teaching about the Holy Spirit in John 16:7-8: *"Nevertheless, I tell you the truth. It is to your advantage that I go away; for if I do not go away, the Helper will not come to you; but if I depart, I will send Him to you. And when He has come, He will convict the world of sin, and of righteousness, and of judgment"* (NKJV).

The Holy Spirit is the gift we receive when we accept Jesus as our personal Savior. What a wonderful thing for the Father to do! Why not stop right now and thank God for this constant Companion, your ultimate accountability partner.

Margaret's Testimony to God's Faithfulness

I am so thankful to God for giving me His precious Holy Spirit. He is "another Jesus" in my life. I first met the Holy Spirit when I was 9 years old. At the time, I did not know His name, but realized that a still, small voice did a huge work in my life, convicting me of my need for Jesus.

After I received Jesus as my Savior, the Holy Spirit of God began His transforming work, gently nudging me to repent when my thoughts, actions, or attitudes did not conform to the image of God.

As I would struggle and then surrender specific areas of my life, one by one, the Holy Spirit would reveal the truth of God's Word to me; and I began to grow in godliness. The Spirit of God delighted me by teaching me the deep things of God found in His Word—things I could never have known apart from Him. I learned to love God's Word; it became life itself to me.

After 23 years of marriage, my husband was diagnosed with a terminal illness and his healing came in heaven. I did not want to go on living. However, the Holy Spirit breathed life and hope back into my lungs and heart as He walked alongside me day-by-day, constantly comforting and assuring me that I would make it, that this loss would even work to make me stronger.

Today, the Holy Spirit remains active in my life as my Guide and Companion, and I welcome Him to hold me accountable!

For His Eyes Only

On page 13, read the poem "Hide and Seek." Are you ready to face a holy God? Why or why not? _____

_____

_____

When you consider areas of need in your life, known only by God and you, what actions do you need to take? Write them here and act on them.

_____

_____

(If one of those needed actions is to accept Him as your Lord and Savior, see p. 127 for steps on making this important decision.)

TALK IT THROUGH

How might knowing that we are required to explain, or otherwise justify, our behavior to God work for our advantage?

_____

_____

_____

_____

_____

_____

_____

_____

Share a personal illustration of how being accountable before God has influenced your behavior.

_____

_____

_____

_____

_____

_____

_____

_____

HIDE AND SEEK
BY CANDY ZARCONE

I think I'm hidden from Your view.
No one will find me, not even You.
I just can't bear for You to see, the ugly, sinful parts of me.

Lord, You're holy, pure and good.
I fear I'll be misunderstood.
How it grips my heart, to risk rejection.
What will You say of my imperfection?

Beginning with fig leaves I tried to hide,
With shallow busyness disguising my pride.
So, I raise my mask of expectation in superficial conversation.

Oh, much deeper I long to go!
I know my heart should be Your home.
Can I let myself be fully known,
Or will fear and mistrust keep me alone?

Why do I think I can hide from You?
Nothing has escaped Your view.
The light came on, bright as day,
Nothing shocks You, You won't turn away.
I surrender my fear, what sweet relief!
Vulnerable and open for You to see.
My disguise is stripped, all is revealed.
In Your perfect love, all is healed.[5]

ACCOUNTABLE TO ONE ANOTHER

When I (Margaret) went away to college my freshman year, I experienced, as many collegians do, a new freedom. Opportunities to alter my Christian goals and commitments constantly challenged me. I soon realized that I still felt compelled to consider how my mother would feel if she knew what I was doing. Some might call that bondage; I call it protection. The sense of feeling answerable to her for my actions, though I rarely gave her a full account, proved to be a valuable safeguard for me.

Read 1 Peter 5:5.

In the *Holman Christian Standard Bible*®, this verse tells us we are to be subject to one another. The Greek word for *subject* is "hupotasso," which means "to place in order, to place in an orderly fashion" as a voluntary choice.[6]

As Christians, we are to willingly submit to the authority of those whom God has placed over us, even in the secular world. How do you think we are required to live out 1 Peter 5:5 in our society? _____

_____

_____

How has voluntary submission benefitted you? _____

_____

The world at large places a high premium on independence, even viewing it as a sign of strength. Sometimes it is easy for believers to buy into this mind-set. Yet in the body of Christ, we are to be interrelated with other Christians.

What does the Bible call this interrelatedness (see I John 1:7)?

_____

_____

The Greek word for fellowship is *koinonia*, which means "to share in, communion or intimate communication."[7] The definition includes the idea of imparting our very selves in the lives of other believers.

Two sometimes destructive opposites can kill the koinonia referred to in 1 John 1:7. One is independence and the other is codependence. *Independent*, according to Webster's Dictionary, includes these definitions: "not influenced or controlled by others in matters of opinion, conduct, etc.; not dependent or contingent upon something else for existence, operation, etc.; not relying on another or others for aid or support. Refusing to be under obligation to others." *Codependent*, the other extreme, means existing solely on the alms or support of another.

Galatians 6:2 and 6:5 steer us away from both behaviors by reminding us that, while we are to bear one another's burdens and so fulfill the law of Christ, each of us is also to bear his or her own load. Galatians 6:2 refers to extra loads, difficulties, or problems that we are to share by helping carry the load. In Galatians 6:5 *load* refers to life's routine obligations that we shoulder for ourselves.

How, then, are we to relate to and closely connect with other women, especially within our small accountability group? We are to be *interdependent*, mutually sharing, giving and receiving, making healthy investments in one another's lives.

According to Ephesians 4:25, we are "members of one another." It is interesting to note that "one another" is defined as one word, treated together. God gives members of His body directives for living through the "one anothers" found in Scripture.

As you read these passages, discover how we are to be mutually sharing in the body. Write a one- or two-word reminder.

First Peter 1:22 _____

Romans 12:10 _____

Romans 15:7 _____

Romans 15:14 _____

Galatians 5:13 _____

Ephesians 4:32 _____

Colossians 3:16 _____

First Thessalonians 5:11 _____

Read and paraphrase Romans 14:7-8. _____

_____

_____

God knows that women need personal intimate relationships with other women, safe places where they can share their souls. As believers, our lives are already intertwined, establishing the close connection that we can strengthen by participating in a small accountability group.

Two examples in nature—the Colorado aspen and the California redwood—beautifully illustrate this connection. The Colorado aspen tree does not grow alone; rather, these trees are found in clusters or groves. Trees send up new shoots from the roots. In a small grove, all of the trees are connected by their roots.

Because the giant California redwood trees tower 300 feet into the sky, they would surely require extremely deep roots to anchor them against the strong winds. Their roots are actually quite shallow, to take in as much surface water as possible. Their roots also spread out in all directions, thus intertwining with those of the trees around them. With their roots locked together, all of the trees support each other in wind and storms.

God intended that we be closely connected in the body of Christ so we can weather the storms while continuing to grow stronger. Collectively we strive as one body to further God's kingdom.

TALK IT THROUGH

What benefits have you received from your connections with your earthly family?

How do these relationships compare to your connection with your spiritual family?

Would you be willing to spend the time and energy to become involved in a small group?

ACCOUNTABILITY ADVANTAGES

This morning as my husband and I (Shirley) were having coffee on our screened-in porch, we noticed a flock of geese flying in V-formation. Geese fly that way for a reason. As each bird flaps its wings, it creates uplift for the bird immediately following. By flying in this formation, the entire flock has a much greater flying range than it would have if each bird were flying solo.

When the lead goose gets tired, it drops back into formation to get the advantage of the uplift, and another one takes its place. When a goose gets sick, is wounded by gunshots, or falls from formation, two other geese follow to lend help and protection. They stay with the fallen goose until it is either able to fly or dies. Only then do the two abandon the fallen goose and join another flock.

What advantages of accountability do you see illustrated by the flying habits of geese? _____

_____

_____

Read Ecclesiastes 4:9-12. What reasons do you discover for accountability?

_____

_____

_____

Describe situations in which you have seen this verse in action. _____

_____

_____

Practical Advantages of Accountability

When we choose to make ourselves accountable to others, we discover some distinct advantages. Check the ones that would be most useful to you.

❑ **When we are accountable, we are less likely to be overtaken by sin.**

Proverbs 11:14: — *"Without guidance, people fall, but with many counselors there is deliverance."*

Proverbs 13:14: — *"A wise man's instruction is a fountain of life, turning people away from the snares of death."*

Proverbs 13:20: — *"The one who walks with the wise will become wise, but a companion of fools will suffer harm."*

Temptation itself is not a sin; it only becomes sin when we yield to it. In what area are you facing the greatest temptation? _____

_____

_____

_____

❑ **When we are accountable, we can better see the big picture.** Most of us race through life much like a horse wearing blinders; we see the path that lies directly in front of us, but remain oblivious to the periphery. Heart Friends not only help us to remove our blinders, giving us a more panoramic view, they also encourage us to sharpen our vision. Then we are more likely to see our blind spots (see Prov. 27:17).

❑ **When we are accountable, we receive spiritual support that can strengthen us.** In every relationship there is a stronger and a weaker vessel. At times I am the stronger vessel, and at other times I am the weaker vessel. I am either in a position to give or to receive support.

Read Romans 15:1-6.

What burdens do you carry that have become too heavy to carry alone? Would you be willing to share the weight with someone in an accountability group? Why or why not? _____

_____

_____

_____

_____

❑ **When we are accountable, we are more likely to maintain balance.**
Life is to be lived in balance, not in extremes.

❏ **When we are accountable, we receive encouragement to reach our goals.**
Assessing individual goals and sharing them with fellow group members can make
us more determined to carry them out.

❏ **When we are accountable, we receive prayer support from others.**
God expects us to pray, even as He knows our needs. We are strengthened
as we intercede for one another.

Read James 5:16, followed by Proverbs 28:13.

Consider a time in your life when you solicited prayer support from another
believer over a particular sin in your life. Did you find it difficult to openly confess
this sin to another? Why or why not? _____

_____

_____

_____

Were the rewards you received from sharing about this sin worth it?

_____

_____

After several years of dealing privately with a personal fear, I (Margaret) openly
confessed it to my accountability group. Many times I had been plagued by this
fear and would cry out to God about it, seeking His help privately but keeping
it hidden from anyone else. I was amazed at the victory that came through my
confession and the prayers of my accountability group.

❏ **When we are accountable, we remain constant in the daily disciplines
of the Christian life—Bible study, prayer, and witnessing**

How do you find yourself struggling with these daily disciplines? _____

_____

_____

_____

How could an accountability partner keep you on track? _____

_____

_____

_____

❑ **When we are accountable, we establish meaningful relationships with others who desire this level of friendship.**

TALK IT THROUGH

Realizing the many advantages of accountability, why would anyone resist it?

_____

_____

_____

_____

_____

The three most commonly expressed fears are:

      Rejection — "If you really knew what I'm like inside, you might not like me."

      Embarrassment — "I've made too many mistakes."

      Loss of control — "I'm independent by nature and do not submit easily."

What fears do you experience as you consider starting an accountability group?

_____

_____

_____

_____

_____

What other concerns do you have that might cause you to resist becoming part of the accountability process? _____

_____

_____

_____

_____

_____

ATTRIBUTES OF AN ACCOUNTABLE PERSON

In a personal accountability group, members are willing to reveal their inner selves. They understand that transparency is the only place to begin if they desire to grow a relationship to a deeper level. Transparency is the "Start button" that must be pushed.

Transparency

Webster's Dictionary defines *transparent* as "having the property of transmitting rays of light through its substance so that bodies situated beyond or behind can be distinctly seen ... easily seen through." So often we hide behind opaque masks, attempting to cover up what is on the inside in an attempt to project a certain image. In doing so, we block the rays that would allow other people to see our "real selves."

The result? Our deepest needs go unrecognized and unmet. We remain isolated, alone, and shallow in our relationships.

Being part of a Heart Friends small group will provide a safe place to learn to let the real you shine. Be patient with yourself and with others, for some members may have worn masks for a long time. The process may be slow and painful. (See "The Paint Brush," p. 32)

Ask yourself: *Am I willing to reveal what God wants to heal in order to gain prayer support and encouragement to grow in godliness?*

Honesty

Honesty may be defined as proclaiming the truth with sincerity and frankness in all situations. Ephesians 4:15 states, *"But speaking the truth in love, let us grow in every way into Him who is the Head—Christ."* The truth we will be speaking will be the truth according to God's Word. That is why it is necessary to be joined together with believers in this small accountability group.

In the world, we may have friends who flatter us, but Heart Friends are honest and speak the truth. It has been said, "The truth will set you free but first it will make you miserable."[8] Heart Friends are those

Be sensitive to fears, real or unfounded, as women consider becoming part of an accountability group. They may express themselves in these ways:

- *"I'm afraid to be known."*
- *"I don't want others to see my true colors."*
- *"We don't always trust each other."*
- *"I'm very private."*
- *"I'm not bold."*
- *"God may ask me to change!"*
- *"Sometimes I am unwilling to change."*
- *"I'm afraid to fail."*

who are willing to speak the truth (about themselves first) and pray you through the misery that may accompany the truth!

Accountability means making yourself vulnerable to a few trusted friends by lowering your defenses and giving these friends the right to examine, question, appraise, and give godly counsel. Such godly accountability requires that you be open and willing to give and to receive truth.

Humility

First Peter 5:5 reads, *"… And all of you clothe yourselves with humility toward one another…"* Humility is having a correct estimate of oneself in comparison to who God is. Humility means that esteeming another person, not as an equal, but as someone of higher regard than myself.

Romans 12:10 tells us to *"be devoted to one another in brotherly love. Honor one another above yourselves"* (NIV). Each member of my accountability group is important to me—so much so that I (Margaret) am committed to her welfare, desiring to see her grow in godliness. Her needs, desires, and concerns have now become mine as well.

Trustworthiness

Heart Friends will be a safe haven for sharing as women grow to trust one another. Each member must pledge to keep confidential anything that is shared within the group. Proverbs 17:9 tells us that *"He who covers over an offense promotes love, but whoever repeats the matter separates close friends"* (NIV). Our desire is to protect our accountability group from scorn and criticism.

Covering over an offense does not mean encouraging someone to continue in sin, but it does mean refusing to expose that weakness openly. Many friendships have been severed by publicly sharing private matters.

Are you willing to allow God to develop these attributes in your life?

TALK IT THROUGH

What are some "masks" women hide behind? _____

_____

What makes dropping a mask so difficult? _____

_____

How would you differentiate between honesty and frankness?

_____

_____

_____

How does having a correct estimate of God bring you to a place of true humility?

_____

_____

_____

How does the way you view yourself influence the way you view others?

_____

_____

_____

_____

Name a time when you "covered" another friend with Christian love.

_____

_____

_____

_____

ACQUIRING AN ACCOUNTABILITY GROUP

Finding a small group of women committed to the same spiritual growth goals is worth taking the time to discern God's leadership. When I (Margaret) recognized my need for an accountability group, I began to ask God to put this same desire on the heart of another Christian woman. It was not long before another woman asked whether I would be interested in belonging to such a group. Tell God about your desire for an accountability group, and patiently follow His leading.

Ask God to prepare your heart.
God may have to reveal your independence before you can become interdependent enough to voice deep needs before a group. Expect God through the Holy Spirit to begin preparing your heart.

As you consider your relationships, can you think of some ways you might become more interdependent? _____
_____
_____
_____
_____

Wait patiently on God.
He may be working in the life of another woman, bringing her to the point of realizing her need for accountability. The delay may be God-designed.

While you wait patiently on the Lord, name two actions you can take to make yourself ready to be an accountability partner.

1. _____
_____
_____
_____

2. _____
_____
_____
_____

When God brings someone to your mind, recognize that this is the time to approach her about being involved in an accountability group.

Allow God the freedom to choose for you.
Your best friend will not necessarily be the right accountability partner for you. Why is this statement true? _____

_____

Keep it small.
The recommended size of an accountability group is three to five members of the same gender who share a mutual desire to grow in godliness.

Test the waters through prayer.
Because prayer is foundational for experiencing God's working in and through individual lives, it is important for the group to be comfortable praying together.

At this point, each person is simply exploring the possibility of establishing an accountability relationship. The decision to commit will come later.

TALK IT THROUGH

Developing real relationships is a process that requires time and effort. Can you share how God knit your heart together with another believer and then caused that relationship to flourish? _____

_____

_____

What factors did you find to be essential in the growth of that friendship?

_____

_____

_____

_____

ACCOUNTABILITY ACTION PLAN

Accountability does not just happen. It does not come quickly or easily because it is a commitment and a process. As is true with any small group, building trust and confidence requires time and effort. These principles can give you the encouragement to work out the specifics your group needs.

Recognize that no two accountability groups will look alike.

Margaret's group is comprised of three middle-aged grandmothers. One is single and works full time as a real-estate agent; one is a dentist's wife and home-maker; and Margaret is involved full time with her speaking and writing ministry, Threads of Hope.

This group meets in the same home every time, sharing a cup of coffee around a kitchen table. After three years of being together, they have come to experience open transparency and honesty as they share their struggles and rejoice over answered prayer.

Shirley's group looks different. All three women are involved in full-time ministry. They meet at 6:30 a.m. in Shirley's home every other week. Occasionally they celebrate victories and meet for breakfast at a local restaurant. These women are growing in godliness as they spur one another on toward love and good deeds.

Another group of young women, wives with small children, chooses to meet on Saturday mornings, twice a month, from 6:30 to 8:00 a.m. They agree to "come as they are." They desire to encourage one another to become godly wives and mothers and to draw closer to the Lord. One of the group members shared this insight: "We spent the first month just peeling away the layers and were strengthened by admitting that none of us 'has it all together.' "

Each group has the freedom to develop its own format, methods, and procedures. You will find that some things work for your group while others do not. Sometimes trial and error is the best way to discover what works best for your group. Each member of the group needs to be open, flexible, and patient during this process. A success story is waiting for you!

Sharing through prayer times is a safe place to begin. We recommend that you individually work through "Accountability Advantages" (p. 17-20), using "Talk It Through" for group participation.

"Safe Starters" for Developing Group Intimacy

1. Use the Personal Goal Worksheet on pages 35-38. Each member should spend time completing this personal assessment, and then share her goals with other members.
2. Write a brief history of your life, recapturing facts about your birth, parents, childhood days, and adult years. Share both the pains and the pleasures you experienced throughout those times.
3. Using the suggested two-minute format on page 39, write your personal testimony of your salvation experience. Share it with your group.

All of these are nonthreatening activities. Feel free to choose one or all to begin the connecting process, and remember there is no right or wrong way to develop your group. Every accountability group develops its own chemistry.

TALK IT THROUGH

Why do we need to begin with "safe starters"? _____
_____
_____
_____
_____

Can you think of additional ways to ease into the introduction phase of an accountability group? _____
_____
_____
_____
_____

Even if group members have been friends for a while, vital relationship account-ability comes almost exclusively from deliberate and intentional effort. Pursue it with the same fervor and energy spent in hunting down a new hairdresser or finding that perfect pair of shoes, for this is much more important.

SUGGESTED MEETING FORMAT AND ACTIVITIES

What does an accountability group actually "look like"? What happens in a typical meeting? are questions you may be asking yourself.

Based on our experiences, the following are typical activities that would occur in a group that meets twice a month. Consider these tips as you begin your own small accountability groups. This sequence follows the format suggested by your Journaling the Journey pages.

❋ **Set a specific time to begin and end your meeting.**
Always begin with a short prayer, asking God to guard your conversation and guide your discussion.

❋ **Rotate leadership so that responsibility is shared among all members.**
No one person is in charge. This is a shared responsibility, not a mentoring or a teaching situation. The facilitator opens in prayer and selects the format for that meeting. To prevent boredom, allow the leader the freedom to vary the course of action for a meeting.

❋ **Ask a Hard Question.**
At this time in the meeting, the facilitator brings a Hard Question to the group's attention. Hard Questions address areas of individual struggle over which a woman is seeking spiritual support and accountability. These questions are designed to help members overcome weaknesses and reach their full potential as women of God.

Each woman selects a Hard Question that reflects her needs or interests (or she personalizes one from the list provided on pp. 81-82). Usually a woman will repeat the same Hard Question until she experiences victory in that area. Then she may move on to select a different Hard Question.

One question should be the focus of discussion each week.

❋ **Using your Journal pages (88-117), record important information shared within the group.**
Margaret's accountability group jots down prayer requests and records our Hard Questions and personal commitments. In the corner in small print—hardly legible—we also indicate our weight! While you don't have to do that, you should find the journal pages helpful for recalling information your group members shared.

⊛ **Review prayer requests from the previous meeting and share praises.**
Celebrate answered prayer and victories since the last meeting.

⊛ **Now comes the time to "Talk It Through."**
One at a time, share personal struggles and needs, always striving to be open and honest. It is important that everyone stay sensitive to the schedule so that each member has a chance to share.

Some struggles expressed in the group will be ongoing, due either to personal failures or to circumstances beyond our control. Being part of a Heart Friends group will afford you the discernment to recognize the difference.

This group should be your encouragers, your loudest cheerleaders. However, frankness in love, not flattery, is a must for the success of all. (See pp. 44-45.)

⊛ **At this point in a meeting, verbalize and record steps of action as a customized commitment.**
Often we find that a personal commitment becomes a shared commitment.

For example, at one meeting, each member of my group (Margaret's) expressed a desire to refocus on a purposeful prayer life. Practicing His presence in prayer throughout the day was not the problem, but stopping long enough to focus entirely on Him was. We committed to pray on our knees daily for a specific amount of time. Our desire was to reestablish the daily discipline of prayer.

However, at another time in our group's life, we realized we were becoming project-prone, too busy, always in a hurry. Our desired commitment at that time was to begin practicing His presence all day long.

One member shared this overwhelming victory at our next meeting: "At one point, I became so engrossed in practicing His presence, that upon getting into my car, I found myself looking over at the passenger seat and saying out loud, 'OK, Jesus, fasten your seat belt!' "

⊛ **Monitor time wisely.**
Save time to close in prayer, just as you opened with a focus on God. Allow each person an opportunity to pray, making sure all needs are addressed by prayer. Carefully give God the glory for the victory in each person's life.

This is a suggested format only. Evaluate your action plan often so that your meetings continue to be energizing, exciting, and challenging for each member in your group.

ADDITIONAL ACCOUNTABILITY QUESTIONS

Do we need to establish an overall purpose for a Heart Friends group?
Every Heart Friends group needs a designated purpose. Establishing one sets the course and keeps individual members on track. For example, Shirley's group developed this purpose statement: "To encourage each other in our daily walk with the Lord to become women of integrity, holiness, and purity." Some groups focus on developing a strong prayer life or becoming consistent in Bible study.

⁑ **Where and when should a group meet?**
Choose a meeting place that offers privacy. It is best to keep the same location—one less decision to make! Sometimes, for variety, we meet at a restaurant.

My group meets in the same home, at the same hour, on the same day every other week. Many groups meet weekly. Commitments seem to wane for groups that meet only once a month. We limit each meeting to 1 1/2 hours.

⁑ **Do members sign a contract?**
Establishing a covenant is more appealing. Even a covenant may seem awkward, but it affords your group a set of ground rules and some structure, thus setting some boundaries within the group. Everyone comes into a Heart Friends group with unspoken assumptions. When members spell out expectations, discuss them, and write them down, they will be on the same page.

⁑ **How do we incorporate the Word of God in our meetings?**
A Heart Friends group is not a mentoring group nor a Bible study group. However, God's Word is the standard and is incorporated in various ways. My group committed to read through the Bible two years in a row using the same reading plan. We hold each other accountable to be consistent in our readings.

⁑ **Should our emphasis occasionally center on outreach?**
A Heart Friends accountability group is meant to help Christian women reach full maturity in Christ, which calls us to have a kingdom focus. Therefore, we encourage women to use their gifts to share the gospel. One question my group poses each time we meet is, "Have you shared the gospel with someone new since we last met?"

❃ **How long would someone typically stay in a Heart Friends group?**
Our suggestion is to set aside three months; then reevaluate and recommit for an additional three months. My group has been together for more than two years, but we renew our commitment often, allowing women the freedom to discontinue should the need arise.

❃ **What steps should the group take if a member does not keep her covenant or loses interest in the group?**
She should be confronted in love and reminded of her covenant agreement. If circumstances in her life have changed, she may need to be given the freedom to leave the group without apology.

❃ **What about child care?**
Mothers of young children may want to think about meeting early on Saturday mornings. Another good time is in the evening when a baby-sitter could care for children in a separate area. Think about meeting at church at a time child care is already in place. Working women may find a lunch meeting helpful.

❃ **Should we stay in touch between meetings?**
In my group, we normally do not call each other unless a prayer request prompts follow-up. But an unexpected encouragement card or e-mail is always appropriate.

❃ **How do we keep accountability groups from becoming cliques?**
In large gatherings, avoid always staying together in a "holy huddle," so to speak. Keep leaders informed about how accountability groups are helping women grow in their faith. Continually be sensitive to other ladies who might want to participate in future groups.

❃ **How does our group ensure that each person has equal time to talk?**
The goal of each meeting is that each group member have ample time to share. Give one another the freedom to call attention to someone who unintentionally dominates the conversation.

As a group use three R's to keep a conversation going: *redirect* the conversation back to the group; *remind* the group of your limited time together; and *reinforce* your love and appreciation for the one dominating the conversation.

THE PAINT BRUSH

LEE EZELL

I keep my **Paint Brush** with me,
wherever I may go, in case I need to cover up,
so the **Real Me** doesn't show.
I'm so afraid to show you **Me**; afraid of what you'll do;
you might laugh, or say mean things;
I'm afraid I might **Lose** you.

I'd like to remove all my **Paint coats**, to show you the real, true **Me**.
But I want you to try and understand: I need you to **Like** what you see.
So, if you'll be patient and close your eyes,
I'll strip off my coats real slow:
Please understand how much it hurts, to let the **Real Me** show.
Now my coats are all stripped off.
I feel naked, bare and cold.
If you still love me, with all that you see,
you are my friend, pure as gold.

I need to save my **Paint Brush**, though, and hold it in my hand:
I want to keep it handy, in case somebody doesn't understand.
So please protect me, my dear friend,
and thanks for loving me **True**.
But, please let me **Keep My Paint Brush** with me,
until **I** love **Me** too! [9]

YOUR
HEART FRIENDS
TOOLBOX

Use the short articles, Conversations
Guides, journaling pages, and other features
in this section just like any other toolbox—
pick and choose items to focus more
specifically on the needs of your group.

Suggested Hard Questions may be selected or
customized from the ones on pages 81-82.

Some features may be helpful for the
leader in personal preparation. Others may
address specific commitments women are
struggling to make.

SETTING PERSONAL GOALS

Putting your purpose on paper will help you discern when life's distractions or demands are forcing you to detour from God's directive. Philippians 1:10 instructs us to *"approve the things that are excellent"* (NKJV). In practical terms, this means learning to prioritize activities and goals. Anything less than a conscious commitment to the important is an unconscious commitment to the unimportant. Then the key to successful living becomes scheduling your priorities accordingly.

Somehow women have been teased, coaxed, enticed, and sometimes even scolded and shamed into believing that "busier is better"—and, as a result, we find ourselves overwhelmed with activities. There is a popular saying: "The hurrier I go, the behinder I get." When we live this way, we end up stressed out, scattering bits and pieces of ourselves everywhere.

Where you are today is largely the result of past thinking and past decisions. Where you find yourself next year at this time will be the result of today's thoughts and decisions.

As children of God through faith in Christ, we have the responsibility of running the race and achieving the goals God has for us. Each believer has a special lane in which to run; each, an individual goal to achieve.

Paul instructs us to walk in wisdom: *"See then that you walk circumspectly, not as fools but as wise, redeeming the time"* (Eph. 5:15-16, NKJV). *Circumspectly* means walking with exactness, keeping your eyes open, and living with purpose each day. *Redeeming the time* generally means "to buy up, to buy all that is anywhere to be bought, and not to allow the suitable moment to pass by unheeded but to make it one's own."[10]

The intentional act of developing a life mission statement and personalized goals for achieving that statement is helpful in living a life of purpose and fulfillment. This action will be an ongoing process in your life, as it is in ours. It is purposeful and intentional, requiring much prayer and personal assessment time before the Lord.

Therefore, do not expect to be able to complete this project quickly or in one setting. You may become overwhelmed if you do. Instead, give God time to show you where He is working in your life, and give yourself ample time to reflect and meditate on your life.

PERSONAL GOAL WORKSHEET

NAME   DATE

MY LIFE PURPOSE OR GOAL:

MY LIFE VERSE (THE VERSE THAT BEST EXPRESSES MY LIFE PURPOSE):

MY ANNUAL VERSE (THE VERSE THAT BEST EXPRESSES MY GOALS THIS YEAR):

MY SPIRITUAL GIFTEDNESS:

MY NATURAL TALENTS:

MY GOD-GIVEN PASSIONS:

MY SIGNIFICANT LIFE EXPERIENCES:

LIFE LESSONS LEARNED FROM THE EXPERIENCE:

MY LIFE PRIORITIES:

SPIRITUAL GOALS:

STEPS OF ACTION I PLAN TO TAKE:

_____

_____

_____

_____

_____

_____

PHYSICAL GOALS:

_____

_____

_____

_____

_____

STEPS OF ACTION I PLAN TO TAKE:

_____

_____

_____

_____

_____

FINANCIAL GOALS:

_____

_____

_____

_____

_____

STEPS OF ACTION I PLAN TO TAKE:

_____

_____

_____

_____

_____

_____

_____

_____

SOCIAL/RELATIONSHIP GOALS:

_____
_____
_____
_____
_____
_____

STEPS OF ACTION I PLAN TO TAKE:

_____
_____
_____
_____
_____
_____
_____
_____
_____
_____
_____
_____
_____
_____
_____
_____
_____
_____
_____
_____
_____
_____
_____
_____
_____
_____
_____
_____

MY PERSONAL TESTIMONY

1. **My life before receiving Jesus:**
   Be able to—*Say in 30 seconds, write in 25 words*

   _____

   _____

   _____

   _____

   _____

   _____

   _____

   _____

2. **How I received Christ:**
   Be able to—*Say in 30 seconds, write in 25 words*

   _____

   _____

   _____

   _____

   _____

   _____

   _____

   _____

3. **My life since becoming a believer:** What is Christ doing in your life right now?
   Be able to—*Say in one minute, write in 50 words*

   _____

   _____

   _____

   _____

   _____

   _____

   _____

   _____

   _____

   _____

CONVERSATIONAL PRAYER
Building trust in and openness to the Holy Spirit

"These all continued with one accord in prayer and supplication, with the women ..."
(Acts 1:14, NKJV). God desires for us to succeed in our Christian walk.
That means that in day-to-day living, victory is possible. Christ Himself
said, *"I have come that they may have life and have it in abundance"* (John 10:10).
Living the victories and the abundant life Jesus came to bring must
begin with prayer.

A good friend of Shirley's, Paula Hemphill, once commented that everything
begins with prayer—and how true her insight is. Prayer is the answer to everything! *"The effectual fervent prayer of a righteous man availeth much"* (Jas. 5:16, KJV)
is a verse many believers can recall from memory; a contemporary wording
reminds us of the impact of prayer: *"The intense prayer of the righteous is very powerful."*
When women start praying in one accord, in the name of Jesus, things begin to
change dramatically—lives, families, churches, and entire communities.

To experience success with Heart Friends, practice this advice: Pray first and
talk later. Any number of prayer techniques might be followed during a Heart
Friends prayer time, but conversational prayer seems to bring closeness to a
group and to invite the presence of the Holy Spirit.

Because an intimate atmosphere is so critical to the success of a small accountability group, consider these guidelines for strengthening conversational prayer.

❋ **Begin group prayer time with individual requests.**
Each woman should take two to three minutes to share her request for that week.
Consistently follow these time limits for prayer requests since starting and ending
on time is crucial to the effectiveness of group meetings.

❋ **Pray about each woman's request.**
There is no set rule regarding who should start. Taking turns leading in prayer
sets a good example for members who are less comfortable praying in public.

❋ **Focus on one subject at a time, learning to pray simple and short prayers.**
In conversational prayer, one person prays aloud while other group members,
pray silently about the same subject. This may take getting used to by some
Heart Friends, but the discipline of staying focused is worth the effort.

When one woman finishes praying aloud, as the Holy Spirit leads, she pauses. This is the signal for another woman to begin (although the one who started praying may pray again later if so led).

⊛ **Become comfortable with the lulls that will occur.**
Conversational-style prayer means to pray as the Holy Spirit leads. Expect pauses while each woman listens to the Holy Spirit. Continually uplift and practice praying as He leads.

⊛ **Close with praise.**
After each woman has prayed matters from her heart, someone should take the initiative to close with praise.

Remember, practice makes perfect. Discipline yourself and equip other Heart Friends to practice conversational prayer and thus reap the full benefits of a praying life.

GUARDING THE CONVERSATION

"I tell you that on the day of judgment people will have to account for every careless word they speak. For by your words you will be acquitted, and by your words you will be condemned" (Matt. 12:36-37) — serious words to keep in mind. Maintaining open, sharing, and praying relationships with other women will help keep you from bottoming out in your spiritual life.

Read James 5:16 to discover the secret to open deep relationships: *"Therefore, confess your sins to one another and pray for one another, so that you may be healed."* Sin is most dangerous to an isolated believer; Satan works best in our lives when we try to keep our sin a secret.

However, God, who has the power over Satan, desires that we have victory over sin. With the help of your accountability group, you can live a life of freedom that is pleasing to God.

Guidelines for Healthy Confession
The following six guidelines can help your Heart Friends develop caring relationships that honor God and one another.

1. Be discreet.
Use care when someone is disclosing the names of people for whom the group is praying. *Always* avoid sharing explicit details and giving endless recitals of someone else's faults.

2. Be sensitive to others.
Limit prayer requests to your immediate family since you have only so much time together as a group.

3. Be honest.
Don't confess someone else's sin. Instead of blaming someone else, focus on the action that is contrary to God's Word. Pray that God would reveal that action to the one for whom you are praying.

4. Be realistic.
Don't expect more from group members than they are able to give. Some issues are best handled by a trained counselor.

5. Be courteous.
Each Heart Friend should have an opportunity to pray. Avoid long or seemingly endless prayers. These courtesies are best understood and agreed upon if addressed when you first meet together.

A healthy group will learn to confront such issues in love. One person who dominates a prayer time can keep the Holy Spirit from moving freely.

6. Be trustworthy.
What is prayed for in the group should remain in the group.

Top 10 Tips for Detecting Gossip in Group Prayer Time
When any of these expressions crop up in your group's conversation, beware. Prayer requests may be turning into gossip.

"I'm not going to give a name, but …"
"I don't know if it's true, but…"
"Have you heard …"?
"I think you need to know …"
"My cousin's brother's wife's …"
"I'll try to make this short …"
"I don't know if you know this, but …"
"We need to pray for the preacher,
  because I heard …"
"Just between us …"
"I really need to tell you …"

Additional Signs of Gossip

❋ *Opinions*
❋ *TMI … Too much information*
❋ *Disclosing personal information
   about others*

More guidelines for conversations that honor God and others may be found in *Conversation Peace: The Power of Transformed Speech* by Mary A. Kassian (© 2001 LifeWay Press).

SPEAKING THE TRUTH IN LOVE

Ephesians 4:15 says we are to speak the truth in love. As a teacher with the spiritual gift of prophesy, I (Margaret) find it easy to speak the truth in love to a large group. Yet I sometimes stumble when faced with speaking the truth in love one-on-one. How do we speak the truth in love in a small accountability group? These six insights can aid in a hard task.

1. Understand what is meant by the word *truth*.
John 17:17 reveals this answer: *"Sanctify them by the truth; Your word is truth."* Truth, then, is that which is from or consistent with God's Word as laid out in the Bible. This excludes our opinions, personal perspectives, or conclusions drawn from our limited human understanding. Shedding light received from a personal experience is helpful but must not be interpreted as the absolute truth.

2. We must be students of the Word to speak the Word.
I find myself falling prey to the temptation to speak my mind rather than the truth of the Word if I am not daily spending time in God's Word. I must be thoroughly equipped in sound doctrine, always striving to *"rightly [divide] the word of truth,"* and avoiding *"idle babblings for they will increase to more ungodliness"* (2 Tim. 2:15-16, NKJV).

We encourage the women in our small groups to search out the Scriptures that apply to their situation and also to be willing to search the Scriptures on behalf of others.

3. Pray for God to give you specific truth for your neighbor.
Ask the Holy Spirit to guide you to this truth. Do not speak truth hastily. God assures us He will give us words for the weary: *"The Lord GOD has given Me the tongue of the learned, that I should know how to speak a word in season to him who is weary. He awakens Me morning by morning. He awakens My ear to hear as the learned"* (Isa. 50:4, NKJV).

Often we feel the urgency to share truth without taking time to hear from God first. Taking time to both search the Scriptures and to hear from God on a matter is wise.

4. Truth must be spoken out of agape love.
If I cannot speak truth in love, I forfeit the right to speak the truth. I recall a time when, in frustration and anger, I blurted out truth to another. My words were spoken harshly and impatiently. Immediately the Holy Spirit convicted me.

Later, a listening friend told me that it was something that needed to be said. However, I had nullified my opportunity to share truth because I had not spoken out of love. *Agape*, or God's love, always seeks the good of another over oneself.

5. Remember the purpose of speaking the truth in love.

The Apostle Paul explains that truth is given explicitly *"for the equipping of the saints for the work of ministry, for the edifying of the body of Christ, ... that we should no longer be... carried about with every wind of doctrine, ... but may grow up in all things into Him"* (Eph. 4:12.14-15, NKJV). Speaking the truth is always for the express purpose of the good of the hearer. We must examine our motive for speaking before allowing words to exit our mouths.

Ephesians 4:25 instructs, *"Putting away lying, 'Let each one of you speak truth with his neighbor, for we are members of one another"* (NKJV). More than simply telling direct falsehoods, lying also includes exaggeration and adding fabrications to something that is true.

In this sense, lying includes the use of flattery, which is an overstated assumption about another person. The motivation of flattery may be to encourage another; but it is not based upon absolute truth and, therefore, *"spreads a net for his feet"* (Prov. 29:5, NKJV). The Book of Proverbs reminds us that a *"flattering mouth works ruin"* (26:28, NKJV) and that *"he who rebukes a man will find more favor afterward than he who flatters with the tongue"* (28:23, NKJV).

6. Speaking the truth in love does not have to be confrontational.

I like to refer to speaking this kind of love as "carefronting." Remember the adage, "People will not care what you know until they know that you care." When truth is spoken in love from the heart, it most likely will be received.

At one point in my life, I was swimming in a sea of self-pity and had no idea why. I thank God for a friend who cared enough to point out that I was consumed with my personal woes. This sharing led to my repentance and restoration and ultimately brought glory to God.

Relationships that are genuine afford us the opportunity to become more comfortable speaking and receiving the truth. However, as one friend in our pilot Heart Friends group learned, long-term friendships do not grant the freedom to speak our minds freely concerning someone else's weaknesses or faults.

UNWRAPPING THE GIFT

Everyone loves to receive gifts! That is what the entire Bible is to each of us—a gift from God with unknown, unlimited delights. But we must handle this gift with care.

Because of its great value, we must help one another handle our gift with the utmost care (see 2 Tim. 3:16-17); but how? We must avoid the temptation to speak hastily, stating only our opinions or thoughts; rather, we must learn to search the Scriptures for truth.

How do we search Bible for specific truths for ourself or for another group member? Use the acrostic *Search* as a guide.

S eek to be silent before the Lord. Always start each Search with prayer.

E xpect to find answers. This will take a little digging. Use your concordance to look up words pertaining to your questions. Dictionaries and commentaries will also help clarify unfamiliar terms.

A sk questions of Scripture. What does the passage or verse say? What is the application to my life? Using other Bible translations will add insights.

R ely on the Spirit. Our relationship with the Lord and the Holy Spirit who lives inside us is so very important when seeking the truth. When we received Jesus as our personal Savior, we received the indwelling Holy Spirit; He will guide us *"into all truth"* (John 16:13).

C haracter counts. The purpose of Scripture is to change us to look more like Jesus. As you search the Scripture, watch to see how our Lord approached a difficult issue. Take note of each characteristic Jesus displayed in a situation. Then ask yourself: *How does this encounter give me direction?*

H ave a teachable spirit. This is a hard one. Allowing the truth to change you can be painful. What better way to accomplish this than with the help of your accountability group! Isn't that why we come together?

Always use God's Word as your standard and you will never go wrong. Pray and love one another. In this kind of atmosphere, God will be glorified and you, my friends, will walk in the truth. Jesus assures us that, *"...you will know the truth, and the truth will set you free"* (John 8:32).

CONVERSATION GUIDES

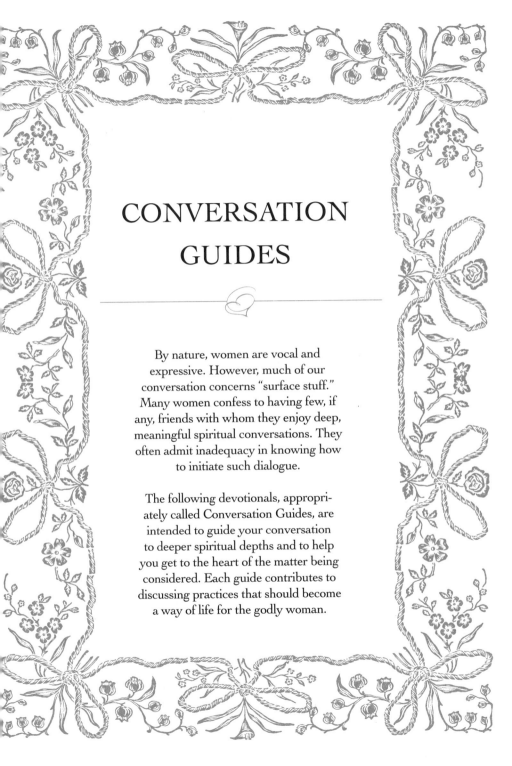

By nature, women are vocal and
expressive. However, much of our
conversation concerns "surface stuff."
Many women confess to having few, if
any, friends with whom they enjoy deep,
meaningful spiritual conversations. They
often admit inadequacy in knowing how
to initiate such dialogue.

The following devotionals, appropriately called Conversation Guides, are
intended to guide your conversation
to deeper spiritual depths and to help
you get to the heart of the matter being
considered. Each guide contributes to
discussing practices that should become
a way of life for the godly woman.

Conversation Guides can be used in the early months of a Heart Friends group, as members learn to open up and trust one another. They can stimulate thought and discussion during meetings. As guides surface needs and struggles, their prayerful use reveals areas in which God is calling members to greater accountability.

We suggest using one Conversation Guide at each Heart Friends meeting. Choose the topic based on the needs of your group or work through guides in order. As you can see, the topics deal with pertinent issues women face today.

GOD'S GOODNESS

GUIDE 1

DATE

How can we ever repay the Lord for everything He has done for us? The psalmist asked the same question—and indicated some ways he would try to do so: *"How can I repay the Lord all the good He has done for me? I will take the cup of salvation and worship the Lord. I will fulfill my vows to the Lord in the presence of all His people"* (Ps. 116:12-14; also see v. 13 in NKJV below).

Repaying the Lord for His goodness can be accomplished in several ways:

* Calling on the name of the Lord
* Keeping our promises
* Being held accountable in the presence of His people

Have you thought of other ways? Share them with your Heart Friends.

_____

_____

_____

_____

Psalm 107:8-9 reads, *"Oh, that men would give thanks to the Lord for His goodness, and for His wonderful works to the children of men! For He satisfies the longing soul, and fills the hungry soul with goodness"* (NKJV).

Specify three ways God has shown His goodness to you.

_____

_____

_____

_____

Close this time with God by writing a prayer to thank God in specific ways for His goodness to you. For example, the psalmist committed to *"lift up the cup of salvation and call upon the name of the Lord"* (v. 13, NKJV).

Would you also agree to practice "thanks-living" by lifting up your full cup, calling upon His holy name, and giving thanks?

_____

_____

_____

2

GUIDE

DATE

CHOOSING TO COMMIT

When faced with a major decision, Ruth made a commitment that shaped the rest of her life. *" 'Don't urge me to leave you or to turn back from you. Where you go I will go, and where you stay I will stay. Your people will be my people and your God my God' "* (Ruth 1:16, NIV).

Answering the call to become a disciple of Jesus always begins with a commitment to follow Him. *"As He was walking along the Sea of Galilee, He saw two brothers, Simon, who was called Peter, and his brother Andrew. They were casting a net into the sea, since they were fishermen. 'Follow Me,' He told them, 'and I will make you fish for people!' Immediately, they left their nets and followed Him"* (Matt. 4:18-20).

Nothing shapes our lives and determines our progress like our commitments. And our commitments can either destroy us or define us as people of character.

Tell me what you are committed to today, and I (Shirley) will tell you the kind of person you will be in 20 years. We live out our commitments by making daily choices. We plan our activities, expend our energy, and give our thoughts to those people and things to which we are committed. Making a conscious commitment to something or someone is the first and most important step toward reaping the rewards of a life lived with purpose.

Do you believe that God truly rewards those who live out their commitments? Why or why not? Explain your answer. _____

_____

_____

_____

_____

_____

List three people or things to which you are committed. _____

_____

_____

_____

Ruth was totally committed to Naomi. The disciples were committed to following Jesus. In both instances, someone took that first step of commitment that leads to a fuller, richer life.

Pray, asking God to give you a heart totally committed to following Jesus with others in your Heart Friends group.

PASSING THE TEST

GUIDE 3

In a broad sense, all of life is a test. We are constantly challenged to develop or reveal what we know, who we are, or what our level of maturity is.

DATE

I (Margaret) had a college professor who gave only one test at the end of the course. Thankfully, God doesn't operate that way! Instead, He daily offers "tests" and watches our responses to the people, pain and problems, successes and failures, disappointments, and even unanswered prayers in our lives. He helps prove or develop our character, fitting us for earthly ministry and heavenly abode.

At the beginning of His earthly ministry, Jesus was tested. We are told that, following His baptism, *"Immediately the Spirit drove Him into the wilderness. He was in the wilderness 40 days, being tempted by Satan. He was with the wild animals, and the angels began to serve Him"* (Mark 1:12-13).

Sometimes we are given a "pop test"; we don't know testing is coming. Often we do not comprehend that we are being tested until after the fact. Our testing is not "standardized"; rather, each test is uniquely and personally designed.

Describe and give a title to one test God has led you through. _____

_____

_____

_____

How would you "score" yourself on that test? _____ %

Being part of a small accountability group is one way God helps us face and handle the tests of life.

What test are you currently undergoing? _____

_____

_____

_____

Share this struggle with your Heart Friends, who will pray for you and offer you godly counsel.

4 GUIDE

HIDING OUR BOO-BOOS

Early on, using their unique baby talk, young children (and sometimes their parents!) describe a minor injury that creates unusual distress as a "boo-boo." Children seems to have an inborn tendency to try to cover a boo-boo or hide it behind their back. Parents beg them to expose the problem and to put a Band-Aid® on it.

Somehow kids believe that hiding a boo-boo will make it go away, and we grow into adulthood still believing that lie. Hebrews 4:13 tells us, *"No creature is hidden from Him, but all things are naked and exposed to the eyes of Him to whom we must give an account."* In your own words, define "naked and exposed."

_____

_____

_____

Consider the eagle's example. When this strong bird eats diseased meat, he will die unless he quickly takes action. He goes to the rock closest to the sun and lies upon it. The rays from the sun literally draw impurities from his body. He remains "spread eagle" before the sun until health is restored.

Scripture teaches, *"He that covereth his sins shall not prosper: but whoso confesseth and forsaketh them shall have mercy"* (Prov. 28:13, KJV). James 5:16 explains how to find help: *"Confess your faults one to another, and pray one for another, that ye may be healed. The effectual fervent prayer of a righteous man availeth much"* (KJV).

After several years of privately attempting to pray and handle a sin of fear, I (Margaret) finally shared it with my accountability group, seeking their prayer support. Sharing my struggle openly helped release me from the power Satan had held over me. In a matter of weeks, I experienced complete victory over this sin.

Are you trying to cover a sin or hide it behind your back? Go to Jesus, our Rock, in open confession, agreeing with Him about your sin. At the same time, share your struggle with your trusted Heart Friends, asking your accountability group to cover you in prayer.

Would you be willing to openly and briefly begin that process?   ❑Yes   ❑No

If yes, write here what you would like Jesus to heal. _____

_____

_____

_____

EARS TO HEAR

GUIDE 5

DATE

I (Margaret) often accuse my husband of having selective hearing — of closing his ears when the words do not seem important or when the subject is not his favorite.

Almost from the beginning of time, God has experienced the same problem with His children: *"Although the LORD sent prophets to the people to bring them back to him, and though they testified against them, they would not listen"* (2 Chron. 24:19, NIV). Likewise, Jesus said, *"He who has ears, let him hear"* (Matt. 11:15, NIV). This admonition is repeated many times throughout Scripture.

What about you? Are your ears trained to hear?   ❑ Yes   ❑ No

According to John 10:27, *"My sheep listen to my voice; I know them, and they follow me"* (NIV). What is evidence that sheep recognize their shepherd's voice?

_____

_____

_____

Although I have never heard God's audible voice, I have learned to recognize when He is speaking. He speaks to me clearly through His Word, through circumstances, and through people. Often, when I am praying about a matter, the Lord will "speak" to my heart in a way that sounds loud in my head. Sometimes a thought so creative and new will suddenly and clearly pop into my mind; I know it is from Him.

Often He instructs me throughout the night (see Ps. 16:7). I awaken with a crystal-clear answer to a problem I had been praying about when I went to sleep.

At other times He brings me a word through another person. However you hear His voice, His answer will always line up with His Word. According to Isaiah 50:5, *"The Sovereign LORD has opened my ears, and I have not been rebellious; I have not drawn back."*

Ask your accountability group members to help you learn to listen for His voice. Sharing what you have heard from Him is a good way to reinforce your listening skills and to help others discern His voice, too.

Share with your Heart Friends one way in which God has recently spoken to you.

_____

_____

_____

6 GUIDE

WEAKER OR STRONGER VESSEL?

DATE

Seeking comfort and advice, I (Margaret) poured out the hurt I had experienced from the hand of another Christian. "How can I continue in this relationship?" My pastor responded, "In every relationship there is always a stronger and a weaker vessel. God always requires more of the stronger vessel than He does of the weaker vessel."

His wise words were based on Romans 15, verses 1 and 2. *"Now we who are strong have an obligation to bear the weaknesses of those without strength, and not to please ourselves. Each one of us must please his neighbor for his good, in order to build him up."* What are the differences in these vessels, based on these verses?

A stronger vessel—This term describes one who is strong in the Lord, grounded in God's love, steeped in Scripture, growing in relationship with Him, and walking in the Spirit.

A weaker vessel—This description might refer to one who is not yet a Christian or to a believer who is still developing mental firmness of character, strength of heart, and a disciplined lifestyle.

Assess the following relationships, marking them *S* or *W* for stronger or weaker:

___Parent ___Child
___Saved ___Unsaved
___Mature Believer ___New Christian
___Student of the Word ___Teacher of the Word

What "more" actions do you think God requires of the stronger vessel? I've suggested one answer; add some of your own in the blanks provided.
More <u>love</u>.

More _____, More _____,
More _____, More _____,
More _____.

Discuss with your Heart Friends the difficult relationships in which you would be considered the stronger vessel. Ask them to pray that God will bring to your mind ways to build up the weaker vessel, especially if you have been hurt.

In the following blank write the initials of one person who comes to mind as a difficult relationship. _____ . Give your group permission to hold you accountable for taking "more" actions in this relationship.

MUD IN MY EYE

GUIDE

7

DATE

Jesus' disciples asked Him about a man blind from birth: *"Who sinned, this man or his parents, that he was born blind?* Jesus answered, *'Neither this man nor his parents sinned. ... [This came about] so that God's works might be displayed in him' "* (John 9:1-3). The description of the encounter continues: *"After He said these things He spit on the ground, made some mud from the saliva, and spread the mud on his eyes. 'Go,' He told him, 'wash in the pool of Siloam' ... So he left, washed, and came back seeing"* (John 9:6-7).

Jesus used the coarse soil of the land to make mud. What do you suppose this mud felt like to the blind man?

_____ welcomed   _____ surprising   _____ comforting   _____ painful
_____ soothing   _____ confusing   _____ strange   _____ an irritant

No doubt, it was irritating! It was bad enough to be blind, but then to have mud rubbed in his eyes added insult to injury!

    Yet the irritant of mud was a tool Jesus used to motivate the blind man to obedience. His personal discomfort (mud in his eyes) was instrumental in bringing about his healing. And the ultimate goal was *"so that God's works might be displayed in him" (v. 3)*.

    Consider some irritants—mud in your eye, if you will—that God may be using to bring about healing in your life and, in turn, glory to Him. Are you experiencing the mud of

    ⊛ loneliness—and, at the same time, the beginnings of a deeper relationship with Him?
    ⊛ a physical hurt—one that is stilling you so you can hear His voice?
    ⊛ financial difficulty—and a greater dependency on Him as a result?
    ⊛ an unruly child—who is forcing you to develop the discipline and practice of praying without ceasing?
    ⊛ an unkind boss—who needs to see the love of God in you?

Share a time God used "mud in your eye" to motivate you to obey Him so that He could bring healing or develop your character for His glory.

_____
_____
_____
_____

8 GUIDE

DATE

FILLED WITH JEALOUSY

"Many signs and wonders were being done among the people through the hands of the apostles. ... Then the high priest took action. He and all his colleagues, those who belonged to the party of the Sadducees, were filled with jealousy. So they arrested the apostles and put them in the city jail" (Acts 5:12,17-18).

Once we grant jealousy a place in our hearts, we find that it soon consumes us, affecting our thoughts and actions. Jealousy and strife usually coexist, causing disorder and evil deeds. *"For where envy and selfish ambition exist, there is disorder and every kind of evil"* (Jas. 3:16).

Have you ever been the victim of someone else's envy? ❑Yes ❑No
How did it lead to disorder? _____
Did you suffer evil treatment? ❑Yes ❑No

Have you ever given jealousy a place in your heart? ❑Yes ❑No
How has jealousy manifested itself in your life?

_____
_____
_____
_____

Margaret: There was a time when jealousy found a place in my heart, tormenting me for a year and bringing about disorder and evil. Although justifiable (in the eyes of some friends), the jealousy monster continued to cause disorder and evil.

One night as I was crying out to God for deliverance, He brought to my mind's eye a picture of myself standing tall in His robe of righteousness. Then I heard His piercing words: "How dare you drape that filthy scarf of jealousy around My precious robe of righteousness." In brokenness and repentance, accepting responsibility for my sin, I resolved to discard the dirty rag I had been wearing for a year.

How could an honest but loving accountability partner have benefitted me during that yearlong struggle? _____

_____
_____
_____

GET STRIPPED DOWN

GUIDE 9

DATE

"Let us lay aside every weight and the sin that so easily ensnares us, and run with endurance the race that lies before us" (Heb. 12:1). To obey this instruction from Scripture, we first must recognize the challenges we face.

The Race = the individual faith-filled life we have been called to complete

Every Weight = any encumbrance that weighs us down

Sin = our tendency to cling to a sinful life

As is the case today, an athlete in biblical times would strip away every piece of unnecessary clothing before competing in a race. He would rid himself of anything that would weigh him down and make it more difficult to run or to endure the preparation of training to run.

List some "weights" in your life.

1. _____
2. _____
3. _____

Due to our natural tendencies, individual temperaments, circumstances, or life experiences, each of us has sins that can easily ensnare us or cling to us. Therefore, we must be on guard against our propensity to sin. List three sins to which you are particularly prone.

1. _____
2. _____
3. _____

After he identified the reality of weights and "ensnaring" sins, Paul essentially told Christians to "get stripped down" for the Christian life, just as an athlete must do for a race (12:1). As believers, we are to lay aside the weights that drag us down and so rid ourselves of the sin that so easily traps us. Our goal is to run with endurance—that steady determination to keep going regardless of the temptation to slow down or give up or take a detour.

Why not give your accountability group permission to "check your dress" for the race that is before you?

10 GUIDE

GOOD DEPOSITS

DATE

Author and Bible study teacher Beth Moore defines New Testament *koinonia* (Christian fellowship) as "expressions of genuine Christianity freely shared among the members of God's family." True koinonia, she says, also may be described as "sharing good deposits."[11] In any level of fellowship, we receive and give as we mutually share.

"And this I pray, that your love may abound still more and more in knowledge and all discernment" (Phil. 1:9, NKJV). Scripture never tells us to love blindly. Instead, we are to love in _____ and all _____.

We are to develop smart hearts.

What would you consider to be some good deposits? _____

_____

_____

_____

Name someone who faithfully makes good deposits in your life. _____

_____

_____

How does he or she do so? _____

_____

_____

_____

Indicate some examples of bad deposits. _____

_____

_____

_____

Right now, why not practice making some good deposits in the lives of your accountability group members?

AVAILABLE AND READY TO SERVE

GUIDE

11

In Ephesians 2:10, Paul tells us what it means to be available and ready to serve: *"For we are His workmanship, created in Christ Jesus for good works, which God prepared beforehand that we should walk in them"* (NKJV).

DATE

Our good works have no part in gaining our salvation but they have a great deal to do in living out our salvation. Good works and service go hand-in-hand in proving a disciple to be genuine.

The phone rings on Sunday afternoon and you check Caller ID. You recognize the number as belonging to your church's Bible study leader. Your know that a facilitator is needed for the Sunday group so you decide to let the answering machine pick up the call. (Of course, no one would ever really do this, would she?)

Life is packed with activity. Each of us struggles to find balance, to find time for family, for friends, and for ourselves. *Where do I find balance among all these demands so that I might do the good works Paul described?* you might ask yourself.

Based on the knowledge that you are *"[God's] workmanship, created ...for good works,"* what are two steps you might take to make yourself ready and available to serve?

1. _____
2. _____

"My Father is glorified by this: that you produce much fruit and prove to be My disciples" (John 15:8). Each of us desires to glorify the Father. When as God's people we do good deeds, they bear fruit for His kingdom and bring glory to His name.

Maybe now would be a good time to ask your Heart Friends to pray that you would always be available and ready to serve.

12 GUIDE

DATE

SINGLE-MINDED PASSION

Where does your mind wander during those moments before you fall asleep? What is the first thing that crosses your mind when you awaken in the morning? Answering these questions honestly can help you discover your greatest passion in life.

Epaphras was a man of single-minded passion and, as such, is a good model for us. The Apostle Paul wrote: *"Epaphras, who is one of you and a servant of Christ Jesus, sends greetings. He is always wrestling in prayer for you, that you may stand firm in all the will of God, mature and fully assured"* (Col. 4:12, NIV).

Epaphras prayed earnestly that the people around him would
1. Stand firm in the will of God,
2. Be mature,
3. Be fully assured.

I (Shirley) wonder what would happen if we were to have such passion and focus. How would this kind of praying truly impact those for whom we dare to pray?

Based on his pattern and his actions, I believe Epaphras' prayer has four characteristics we should consider for ourselves:
1. *A commitment to pray*—A fruitful prayer life begins with a choice, just like Epaphras made.
2. *A time to pray*—Protect that divine appointment at all costs.
3. *Stillness of heart* —If you are too busy to pray, you are too busy.
4. *Sincerity of heart*—Ask God to break your heart for the women in your church.

My challenge for you is to live out the same kind of single-minded passion. For whom will you pray the Epaphras prayer? Write the name of one person God brings to your mind: _____ .

Ask your Heart Friends to hold you accountable to pray for this person for a determined length of time. Indicate that time here: _____ .

HELP, I'M STRESSED OUT!

GUIDE

13

DATE

Do you ever feel like you need to be rescued? Do you have a safe place, a refuge, in which you can hide?

According to Psalm 31:1-3, you do have such a place: *"In you, O Lord, I have taken refuge; let me never be put to shame; deliver me in your righteousness. Turn your ear to me; come quickly to my rescue; be my rock of refuge, a strong fortress to save me. Since you are my rock and my fortress, for the sake of your name lead and guide me"* (NIV).

Not long ago I (Shirley) was feeling stressed out all the time. I found myself pouring my heart out to the Lord for a safe place. I found myself deep in a world of overload. Stress is of the world, not of God, and I had fallen into its trap.

Once during that time, as I was looking out my office window, I saw two birds perched on a high wire, singing without a care. I asked the Lord how they could be so carefree when they were living in the same stress-filled world! It dawned on me that it was my perspective that was affecting how I saw the world. *O, Lord, how do I change my perspective?* I cried out.

Then, as if I had been separated from the world for just an instant, God's instruction came to me so clearly: *"Do not conform any longer to the pattern of this world, but be transformed by the renewing of your mind"* (Rom. 12:2, NIV).

Are you feeling trapped? The solution is twofold: you have a part, and God has a part. God revealed His part in Psalm 31. Now it is your turn.

Share with your Heart Friends how you will do your part. _____

_____

_____

_____

_____

_____

Now thank God for His faithfulness to do His part. _____

_____

_____

_____

_____

14 | GUIDE | DON'T LEAVE HOME WITHOUT IT!

DATE

Oh, me! It is almost noon and I haven't had my Quiet Time! Have you ever thought something similar? In the minds of some, a quiet time is a duty—do your duty and receive God's blessings. To others, it is a sign of spirituality—the longer, the better. But to God, a quiet time is an opportunity to take you from ordinary living to abundant living.

In John 10:10 Jesus tells us, *"I have come that they may have life and have it in abundance."* In the Greek the word for abundance, *perissos,* actually means "far more, exceedingly and beyond measure"[12]—not ordinary, but more than we ever could ask for. Now, that is something to get excited about!

God makes known His desires for our lives as He speaks in our quiet times and daily experiences. And those desires lived out bring about abundant life.

What are your God-planted desires? _____

_____

_____

_____

_____

_____

What words come to your mind to describe your time with God? _____

_____

_____

_____

_____

_____

Discuss as a group how each member spends time with God. Note any suggestions you might want to incorporate into your own daily quiet time.

_____

_____

_____

_____

_____

A DIVINE PLAN

GUIDE
15

Thank God that He always has a plan for our lives.

DATE

One passage of Scripture very dear to my (Shirley's) heart speaks of God's divine plan: *"The Spirit told Philip, 'Go to that chariot and stay near it.' Then Philip ran up to the chariot and heard the man reading Isaiah the prophet. 'Do you understand what you are reading?' Philip asked. 'How can I,' he said, 'unless someone explains it to me?' ... Then Philip began with that very passage of Scripture and told him the good news about Jesus"* (Acts 8:29-31,35, NIV).

What an awesome God we serve! He looked down from heaven, saw an Ethiopian eunuch, and provided a way for him to come into a saving relationship. In the same way, no matter who we are or where we are, God finds us and provides a way for us to know Him.

Let's think about God's divine plan in relation to this biblical story. First, there was a man who was searching for truth. Second, there was a man who was willing to share the truth. God is looking for men and women who are willing to be part of His divine plan. Will you join Him?

List three qualities necessary for you to be a woman who is ready to share the truth.

1. _____
2. _____
3. _____

One quality you may have listed is *boldness* (or a similar word). God will give us the ability to be bold, but we must trust Him to lead us in that boldness. *"But you will receive power when the Holy Spirit comes on you; and you will be my witnesses in Jerusalem, and in all Judea and Samaria, and to the ends of the earth"* (Acts 1:8, NIV).

Discuss with your Heart Friends group where your Jerusalem might be; then pray for one another, that you would be women God can count on to be part of His divine plan.

16 GUIDE

DATE

A FRESH START

When is the last time you prayed a prayer similar to this one? "OK, Lord. Today I will have a fresh start. With your help, maybe I can eat well and take care of my body throughout the day. But, Lord, I need your *supernatural God power* to do this."

First Corinthians 6:19 reminds Christians how much God values our bodies: *"Do you not know that your body is a temple of the Holy Spirit, who is in you, whom you have received from God? You are not your own"* (NIV).

Recently my husband and I (Shirley) were invited to our pastor's home for dinner and I was asked to bring dessert. In fact, I was asked to bring two desserts—a coconut pie and a chocolate cake. (Why is it that every time you decide to go on a diet someone invariably invites you to dinner?)

The pie was completely eaten but some of the chocolate cake remained. I didn't want to throw it away; after all, I don't like to waste good food. So I took the cake home. Bad idea!

The next day that cake and I had many struggles and conversations. All day it "called" out to me; every time I turned around I could see that cake. *Enough,* I thought. About 11 o'clock I moved it out of sight, to the laundry room! After lunch I decided to do some laundry. Of course, there sat the cake. And, yes, by this time, I felt as if the cake were watching me!

It is not easy to take care of our bodies, but *"God is faithful; he will not let you be tempted beyond what you can bear. But when you are tempted, he will also provide a way out so that you can stand up under it"* (1 Cor. 10:13, NIV).

Do you struggle with taking care of your body, God's temple? If there are some health areas in which you need a fresh start, talk about them with your Heart Friends. As you are discovering, your Heart Friends offer acceptance and affirmation, but they also help you maintain accountability. Your body will love you for it!

Take a few minutes and write about what your "temple maintenance" looks like.

_____

_____

_____

_____

_____

_____

A PLACE OF COMMON PURPOSE

GUIDE

17

I love the church! It is not just a place where I (Shirley) go on Sundays. It is not just an opportunity to visit with Christian friends. Because it is made up of God's people, the church is a setting in which I can love and be loved in return. I can serve and be served.

DATE

Most important, I know I will receive doctrinal teaching and hear the counsel of God at church. Where else can you go and be offered so much?

The writer of Hebrews had similar understandings when, under the guidance of the Holy Spirit, he wrote: *"And let us consider how we may spur one another on toward love and good deeds. Let us not give up meeting together, as some are in the habit of doing, but let us encourage one another—and all the more as you see the Day approaching"* (Heb. 10:24-25, NIV). These verses suggest mutual responsibility as we face our common task as Christians.

What is that task? To help one another and stand for the cause of Christ. We all could use some help with that one!

How do you think the early church lived out these verses? _____

_____

_____

_____

_____

_____

How do you see your church living out this passage? _____

_____

_____

_____

_____

_____

Discuss with your Heart Friends how you might live out this instruction more intentionally. Ask them to pray for you as you seek to do your part in your church.

18

DATE

WHATCHA THINKIN'?

No matter where I (Shirley) travel, I rest assured that someone will ask, "What part of Texas are you from?" Yes, I must admit that we Texans talk a bit funny at times! Things like "Whatcha thinkin'?" and "I'm fixin' to..." seem to come out of my mouth without thinking.

The thought process is a must for Christians. God commands people to think, as illustrated by His comment to rebellious Israel: *"Come now, and let us reason together"* (Isa. 1:18, NKJV). I am in awe that the Almighty Creator would want to reason (think) with me. Similarly the psalmist cried out, *"Give me understanding, that I may observe Your law and keep it with all my heart"* (Ps. 119:34, NASB).

As believers, we must discipline our minds to think about spiritual realities. In Philippians 4:8, Paul lists (and we highlight) eight godly virtues on which to concentrate: *"Finally, brothers, whatever is <u>true</u>, whatever is <u>noble</u>, whatever is <u>right</u>, whatever is <u>pure</u>, whatever is <u>lovely</u>, whatever is <u>admirable</u>—if anything is <u>excellent</u> or <u>praiseworthy</u>—think about such things"* (NIV, *emphasis added*).

The key to godly living is godly thinking. Solomon wisely observed, *"Watch over your heart with all diligence, for from it flow the springs of life"* (Prov. 4:23, NASB).

Now might be a good time to evaluate your thought life using the checklist from Philippians. Circle the virtues that seem difficult for you to develop as you seek a pure thought life.

True	Noble	Right
Pure	Lovely	Admirable
Excellent	Praiseworthy	

Now ask your Heart Friends to hold you accountable for the steps you will take to change your way of thinking. Take time to write down your plan of action. *Seeing your plan of action in writing will help you remain accountable!*

_____

_____

_____

_____

CULTIVATING GODLY GIRLFRIENDS

GUIDE **19**

DATE

It was 6:30 in the morning and I (Shirley) heard a familiar knock at my back door. One of my Heart Friends had arrived for what I knew would be a sweet time with my accountability group. As she entered the room, I could sense that things were not as they should be.

"Please sit down. Would you care for some coffee?" I asked.

"No. I am just fine, thank you!" came the reply. As the saying goes, you could have cut the tension with a knife.

Only a few minutes passed before I heard another knock at the back door. Startled, I jumped quickly out of my chair. "Come in," I yelled. It was our other accountability group member.

Although I was happy that the three of us were finally together, I wondered what was wrong with my friend. Shortly after we began talking, we came to the heart of the problem. I asked whether she would like to open our group in prayer, to which she replied, "I just don't feel like praying this morning."

I had mixed emotions. I was surprised, but pleased that we had finally come to the point where we could be transparent with each other. This transparency helped the three of us to grow closer that morning. After many tears, we were able to help our friend see God's hand at work in her life.

Friendship is one of the things women "do" best. We love to talk and visit as we seek to deepen our relationships. However, godly girlfriends do not come easily. However, as we learn to share our strengths and our weaknesses, we become increasingly transparent.

Yes, it takes courage to let the *real you* show through. But the results are godly girlfriends, true friends who are there for a lifetime, friends who will always look for ways to put a caring heart into action. Praise God for godly girlfriends!

"A friend loves at all times, and a brother is born for adversity" (Prov. 17:17, NKJV). How would you describe a godly girlfriend?

_____

_____

_____

_____

_____

_____

Has someone been a godly girlfriend to you?   ❑ Yes   ❑ No
If so, write her name here. _____

Using a Bible concordance, look up five Scriptures on the subject of friends or friendship. Be prepared to share what you learned with your Heart Friends. I have given you one example.

Friends give earnest counsel: Proverbs 27:9

1. _____
_____
_____
_____

2. _____
_____
_____
_____

3. _____
_____
_____
_____

4. _____
_____
_____
_____

5. _____
_____
_____
_____

It is our hope and prayer that you will cultivate godly girlfriends within your Heart Friends group.

CEREAL-BOX GIVER

GUIDE

20

DATE

I (Margaret) joined a women's investment club to educate myself on financial and investment matters so I could "get in on" what was happening in the economic world and experience gain in that area. Did you know that God invites you to "get in on" His economy today so that you can experience gain in your personal life?

Jesus had a lot to say concerning kingdom investments: *"Give, and it will be given to you: good measure, pressed down, shaken together, and running over will be put into your bosom. For with the same measure that you use, it will be measured back to you"* (Luke 6:38, NKJV).

What paradox is stated here? _____

_____

Have you ever felt slighted when, upon opening a new box of cereal, it appeared to be only half full? The manufacturer should have shaken the cereal down until it was packed together tightly, and then refilled that box—all the way to the top! In a sense, Luke 6:38 encourages us to be "cereal-box givers"—generous givers.

How can we practice "cereal-box giving"? _____

_____

Would God consider you to be a cereal-box giver? Why or why not? _____

_____

_____

We receive in direct proportion to our: *(check one)*
____ Ability to give   ____ Financial status   ____ Giving

What is the secret to "getting in on" God's economy? _____

_____

_____

Share a time when you experienced a great return on an investment you made in God's kingdom.

21 GUIDE

LOSING YOUR HEAD

When someone loses her temper easily, we say she is prone to "fly off the handle." This common expression refers to the head of a hammer coming loose from its handle as a carpenter is attempting to use it.

Such a mishap renders
- ❀ The hammer useless, no longer good for work.
- ❀ Damage to anything or anybody standing in its path.
- ❀ A need for repairs, of both the hammer and of the damage done.

Now apply this analogy to the Christian walk. When she "flies off the handle," a Christian woman
- ❀ **Loses some effectiveness.** Anger consumes her mind and depletes her energy, rendering her incompetent and unproductive.
- ❀ **Inflicts injury.** Sometimes causing physical injury, anger always inflicts emotional damage.
- ❀ **Feels the effects of her anger.** The person receiving the brunt of her anger rarely recovers quickly, often carrying scars and pain for a long time.

Look over this checklist of forms of anger. Mark those with which you struggle.

_____ malice	_____ envy	_____ wrath	_____ fury
_____ bitterness	_____ seething	_____ hate	_____ irritation
_____ rage	_____ displeasure	_____ impatience	_____ annoyance

How is anger the root cause of these manifestations? _____
_____

Proverbs 22:24-25 (NKJV) instructs, *"Make no friendship with an angry man, and with a furious man do not go, lest you learn his ways and set a snare for your soul."* What warning does this verse give? _____
_____

How does recognizing and confessing the temptation to become angry help prevent us from inflicting pain and causing damage? _____
_____

Next time you are tempted to fly off the handle, think first, take a deep breath, and pray. Choose to "keep your head on straight," knowing God will help you.

TWIN THIEVES

In Conversation Guide 14 we looked at John 10:10, where Jesus teaches, *"I have come that they* (you!) *may have life and have in abundance."* In the same verse in the same translation (HCSB), He describes how the enemy, the thief, comes to _____, _____, and _____.*

DATE

What-ifs and If-onlys are twin thieves the Enemy uses to rob us of the joy of abundant living. Once we are a child of God's, he can do nothing about our eternal security. Therefore, he delights and determines to destroy our day-to-day joy by feeding us fearful thoughts of the unknown future and remorseful and shameful regrets about our unchangeable past.

What-ifs: *Fearful thoughts about the unknown future*
* The majority of the things we worry about never occur.
* There are no What-ifs to God. He knows all and sees all.
* Some psychologists suggest we have five seconds to refute a thought.
* Any sentence that begins with a question mark should be examined for the fear factor.

Share some What-ifs the Enemy is attempting to use with you: _____
_____
_____

If-onlys: *Thoughts or feelings that produce guilt, pain, or shame*
* First John 1:9 assures us that God *"is faithful to forgive us our sins and to cleanse us from all unrighteousness."*
* We must receive God's forgiveness and leave it in the past.
* We cannot change our past.
* We can alter the effect the past has on our present.

List some If-onlys the Enemy is attempting to use in your life: _____
_____
_____

Are you plagued by What-ifs or If-onlys? Why not share these with your account-ability partners, seeking their prayer support and encouragement?

*(steal, kill, destroy)

23 GUIDE THE FEAR FACTOR

DATE

Webster's Dictionary defines *fear* as a "distressing emotion aroused by impending pain, danger, and evil, whether real or imagined; to have reverential awe, especially toward God." As defined here, fear can be either healthy or unhealthy so it is wise to face our fears.

Healthy fears motivate us to take positive steps of action. For example, my awe of God moves me to obey God. My fear of a car accident prompts me to obey laws and wear a seat belt. Fear of catching a cold motivates me to dress warmly.

Unhealthy fear is a paralyzing emotion that triggers negative thought patterns, breeding anxiety, and worry that can multiply like a giant snowball. Fear is like an icy flame. It freezes us into inaction and forms an igloo all around, restricting normal feelings of love, confidence, and well-being. Unless we face unhealthy fear, it will immobilize or cripple us.

Read the following verses to find the effects of fear:

> Proverbs 29:25   Fear is a _____.
> First John 4:18   Fear carries _____.
> Luke 21:26   Fear causes our hearts to _____. *

The temptation to bow down to fear will always be present, but the Word of God tells us to "fear not." Read the following verses to discover how it is possible to live apart from the controlling effects of fear:

> Jeremiah 1:18   God has made you ___ _____ _____.
> Second Timothy 1:7   God has not given you a spirit of
> _____ but of power.
> Isaiah 35:4   God will come and _____ ____. **

Perhaps you need to confront an unhealthy fear, openly confess it before God, and share it with your accountability group. Your Heart Friends will pray for you, thereby disarming the Enemy, who loves to deal in darkness.

* snare, punishment, faint (HCSB)
** a fortified city, featfulness, save you (HCSB)

DAILY DISCIPLINES

DATE

The story is told of a young man who approached the foreman of a logging crew and asked for a job. "That depends," replied the foreman. "Let's see you fell this tree."

The young man stepped forward, and skillfully felled a tree. Impressed with his ability, the foreman exclaimed, "You can start on Monday."

Monday, Tuesday, Wednesday, Thursday rolled by. Thursday afternoon the foreman approached the young man and said, "You can pick up your paycheck on the way out today."

Startled, the young man replied, "I thought you paid on Friday."

"Normally, we do," said the foreman, "But we're letting you go today because you've fallen behind. Our daily felling charts show that you've dropped from first place on Monday to last place today."

"But I'm a hard worker," the young man objected. "I arrive first, leave last, and even work through my coffee breaks!"

The foreman, sensing the young man's integrity, thought for a minute and then asked, "Have you been sharpening your ax?"

The young man replied, "No, sir, I've been working too hard to take the time for that!"

Sometimes we get so busy that we do not take time to "sharpen our axes." Although hard work and service are commendable, we will become dull and lose our effectiveness if we do not take the time to sharpen the ax.

Staying sharp requires practicing daily disciplines. Rate your sharpness from 1 *(low)* to 10 *(high)* in the following:

_____ Prayer
_____ Bible study
_____ Witnessing
_____ Service
_____ Quiet time
_____ Praise and worship

Why not solicit the prayer support of your accountability partners as you commit to spend more time sharpening your ax?

25 GUIDE

SIFTING

DATE

"Do not be hasty to speak, and do not be impulsive to make a speech before God ... let your words be few" (Eccl. 5:2). What advice can you gain from this scriptural warning?

The trouble with the one who talks too fast is that she often says something she hasn't thought of yet! We would be wise to give our words "travel time" — sufficient time to slowly make their way from our hearts to our mouths. The result would be fewer spoken words.

Hanging on my (Margaret's) kitchen wall is a prized possession — my grandmother's sifter. In a flash, my grandmother could turn coarse flour into the softest mountain of white fluff, producing some mighty fine biscuits. She kept that sifter in a handy spot because she sifted flour three times a day.

This verse from Ecclesiastes teaches us to sift our words carefully and often, allowing only the ones that are fruitful and uplifting to be uttered. I have discovered it is not the words I have swallowed that cause me grief, but the ones I have spoken. Often I pray, "Lord, fill my mouth with worthwhile 'stuff' and nudge me when I've said enough."

What characteristics of "edible" words are described in Ephesians 4:29?

_____

Describe "unpleasant" words using the same verse. _____

_____

_____

Check the descriptions that best describe your words:

_____ hastily spoken	_____ well sifted	_____ unwholesome talk
_____ helpful	_____ slowly uttered	_____ helpful for building up
_____ beneficial to others	_____ chosen and few	

With the help of my Heart Friends, I will take these steps to improve:

1. _____

_____

2. _____

_____

3. _____

_____

A TRIP TO THE ROCK

GUIDE 26

DATE

Psalm 61:2 tells us what to do when our hearts are burdened to the point of breaking: *"From the end of the earth I will cry to You, when my heart is overwhelmed; lead me to the rock that is higher than I"* (NKJV).

Oddly enough, the majestic eagle gives us some guidance as well. This bird begins each day with a process called preening. He sits on a high rock and passes each of his wing feathers through his beak as he exhales and breathes on each one. In this early morning ritual, he is "steam-cleaning" his feathers, restoring them from the previous day's activities.

As he breathes on the feathers, a gland in his mouth secretes an oily liquid that seals the individual feathers together, waterproofing them and preparing them for the tasks ahead. This protection is necessary if an eagle is to move through wind and rain or swoop into water to seize food.

If we are to be "steam-cleaned" from yesterday and covered and equipped for whatever God has planned for today, we, like the eagle, must begin our day with a little preening. We must go to the Rock, who is Jesus, and spend time with Him alone, asking Him to "steam-clean" and "waterproof" us. It is for our good and the good of those around us that we are invited to come into His presence at the beginning of every day.

Time alone with the Father was necessary for Jesus to understand the will of the Father and to prepare for ministry. While ministering throughout Galilee, *"Jesus observed this practice: when it was day, Jesus departed and went into a deserted place"* (Luke 4:42, NKJV).

In 1 Samuel 30:6, David, when he was about to be stoned by the people, withdrew to be alone with the Lord and *"... strengthened himself in the LORD his God"* (NKJV).

What sacrifice would you need to make to start your day with a trip to the Rock?

_____

_____

Whether you are like the lark that awakens with a zest and a song, or like a night owl, God has some directives for your day, and He is anxious to share them with you. After all, the One who keeps us does not slumber or sleep (see Ps. 121:3). He has been waiting all night to visit with you!

27 GUIDE

INTERNAL JOGGING

DATE _____

Whenever I (Margaret) pass a jogger, I check out his or her facial expression. I have yet to see one who smiles! Perhaps joggers would be more health-oriented to practice that "internal jogging" known as laughter.

Personally, I find myself to be my greatest source of entertainment! In these later years, I am learning to take myself a lot less seriously. My husband and I were way too serious; so God gave us two sons with a great deal of laughter in their souls. God meant for these two parents to lighten up.

According to Ecclesiastes 3:1-4 there is a time for everything and a season for every activity under heaven, including *"a time to laugh"* (v. 4). Proverbs 31:25 reminds us that the virtuous woman, clothed with strength and dignity, is able to *"laugh at the days to come"* (NIV). Proverbs 16:20 states, *"Whoso trusteth in the LORD, happy is he"* (KJV). Christians, of all people, have reason to be people of joy and laughter. And it should show on our faces!

Many years ago, Norman Cousins was diagnosed as terminally ill and given 6 months to live, with a 1 in 500 chance of recovery. He decided to make an experiment of himself by practicing laughter. He rented funny movies, read funny stories and asked his friends to call whenever they did something funny.

His pain was so great he could not sleep. Laughing for 10 solid minutes, he found, relieved the pain for several hours so he could sleep. He fully recovered from his illness and lived another 20 happy, healthy, and productive years. The journey of this miraculous recovery is detailed in Cousins' book *Anatomy of an Illness*.

Laughter is a luxury that is free and contagious. I have a doll that giggles when you squeeze her tummy. It never fails to bring a smile to my grandchild's face and, in turn, to my own.

When my family gathers, the house seems to vibrate with laughter because we enjoy good, clean fun. As I look back, I thank God for fun-loving children, wishing I had laughed even more often than I did.

When was the last time you laughed out loud with your family? _____

_____

_____

_____

Try maintaining your health through daily doses of internal jogging!

ALLOWING ROOM FOR MARGIN

GUIDE

28

DATE

As a typing teacher, the first thing I (Margaret) taught my students was how to set the margins on their typewriter. I realize this story dates me! Now, years later, I am still learning and stressing the importance of leaving adequate space for margin—not on paper, but in my personal life.

In *The Overload Syndrome* (NavPress) Richard Swenson defines *margin* as the space between our load and our limit.

Whenwe filleverywakingmomentwith activities,we areunabletoclearlyseewhatis importantandwhatisnotimportant. Our lives can look just like this sentence when we neglect to allow proper space between our load and our limit.

We all believe we have so much discretionary time; but, when polled, people end up indicating otherwise. According to some surveys, Americans today sleep fewer hours each night than people did 100 years ago. The average workweek is longer now than it was in the 1960s. The average office worker has nearly a week's worth of work piled up, and it takes us nearly half a day to sort through it!

By some estimates, we spend more than half a year opening junk mail and up to *two years* of our lives playing phone tag with people who are busy or are not answering. When it all adds up, we may spend years waiting for people who are trying to do too much and are late for meetings.

What's the solution? Restore margin to your life. Here are some suggestions for restoring margin to overloaded, overcrowded lives. Check the ones that would be good goals for you.

- ❏ Learn to say no more than yes.
- ❏ Deal honestly with your motives and values for doing more.
- ❏ Stop comparing yourself to others—what they have, what they achieve, how fast or long they work, the money they earn.
- ❏ Concentrate on becoming rather than doing what God desires.
- ❏ Refuse to allow others to dictate and determine your priorities.
- ❏ Schedule margin time in your day just like you would schedule an important meeting.
- ❏ Recognize that your relationships need personal, undivided attention. Ask God to show you where you need to make these adjustments.

Why not ask your Heart Friends how they restore margin in their lives?

A BALCONY OR A
BASEMENT PERSON?

In this world, we encounter two types of people: "basement people"
and "balcony people."

DATE

Basement people are evaluators, analyzers, and often criticizers who freely
offer negative, fault-finding comments; remarks that leave you feeling deflated,
somewhat rejected, less than valuable, as if you did not measure up to certain stan-
dards. Basement people speak words that leave you feeling wounded, crippled, or
damaged. Basement people seem to pull you down ... down ... down.

Balcony people are encouragers who believe in you, boost you up, see positive qualities in you, picture a future for you—and tell you so.

Picture yourself standing in the center of a stage. You see a balcony filled
with people who are not passively observing you, but are on their feet, hanging
over the rail, and waving their hands in the air. Some are applauding, while others
are shouting words of acclamation and encouragement, cupping their hands like a
cheerleader with a megaphone.

Words such as "I always knew you could," "Don't give up," "God has a plan
and a future for you," and "Keep up the good work" come from balcony people.
No doubt you feel yourself smiling, being renewed with a surge of strength that
will cause you to stretch far beyond your self-imposed limits. Balcony people lift
you up ... up ... up.

_____ was/is a balcony person in my life because he/she

_____.

First Peter 3:9 tells us we are called to render blessings so that we in turn might
inherit a blessing. The Greek word for bless, _eulogeo_, means "to speak well of." [13]

My (Margaret's) accountability partners are two of my balcony people. They
speak well of me and they speak truth to me, believe in me, and encourage me to
grow in godliness.

However, the most important questions are these: In whose balcony would
I be found? _____

_____

_____

And do others consider me to be a balcony person or a basement person?

_____

TRUTH OR CONSEQUENCES

GUIDE 30

Have you ever heard someone say, "Oh, it was just a little white lie," or "No harm will come of that," or "It won't hurt anyone"?

This was the type of thinking that overcame Ananias and Sapphira.

DATE

"Now a man named Ananias, together with his wife Sapphira, also sold a piece of property. With his wife's full knowledge he kept back part of the money for himself, but brought the rest and put it at the apostles' feet" (Acts 5:1-2, NIV).

Peter made it clear to Ananias that holding back part of the money was not a sin: *"Didn't it belong to you before it was sold? And after it was sold, wasn't the money at your disposal?"* (Acts 5:4, NIV).

What, then, do you see as Ananias' sin? _____

_____

_____

It is so easy to rationalize our actions. No doubt, this is what happened to this believing couple. Yes, Ananias and Sapphira were believers.

Rationalizing sin always starts with Satan. Peter confronted Ananias in this way: *"Ananias, how is it that Satan has so filled your heart that you have lied to the Holy Spirit ..."?* (Acts 5:3, NIV). Ouch! The truth revealed.

If you answered that Ananias' sin was lying to the Holy Spirit, you are correct. Ananias was surely tempted by Satan, but responsibility for the sin rested on Ananias. He had the freedom to do what he wanted, as do we. The question for Ananias (and for each of us) became, What choice will we make?

Every decision we make brings definite consequences. What will those consequences look like? There are no such things as little white lies that hurt no one. In Ananias' case, the consequences were dire: *"When Ananias heard this, he fell down and died"* (Acts 5:5, NIV).

Start this day fresh, asking God's forgiveness for any so-called little white lie with which Satan has tempted you. Writing it down makes it easier to recall and confess to God. _____

_____

_____

Praise God for His Holy Spirit that dwells in each of us. He is truly our ultimate accountability partner. Scripture reminds us, *"Since we live by the Spirit, let us keep in step with the Spirit"* (Gal. 5:25, NIV).

Now might also be a good time to write out a prayer thanking God for the Holy Spirit who dwells in you.

_____

_____

_____

_____

_____

_____

_____

_____

_____

_____

_____

_____

_____

_____

_____

_____

_____

_____

ASKING THE HARD QUESTIONS

In Psalm 139:23-24, David asks God to do an "inspection" of his heart; he gives God permission to shine His holy flashlight in all the crevices and corners. David prays, *"Search me, O God, and know my heart; try me, and know my anxieties; and see if there is any wicked way in me, and lead me in the way everlasting"* (NKJV). In this psalm, David holds himself up for God's close scrutiny because he desires to walk rightly before God.

As we also seek to rid ourselves of any hint of unrighteousness, we too must be willing to practice open accountability before God. How can we develop such a consistent walk? First, we allow God to search our hearts; second, we respond to the area of weakness, temptation, or blatant sin that He reveals. And third, we ask God to convict us each time this attitude or action rears its ugly head.

How can Heart Friends help? Each member chooses a Hard Question that relates to an issue God reveals; she may either use the following list of questions or suggest one of her own. She willingly shares the question with her group, soliciting prayer support and giving others permission to check her on the matter by restating the question at the next meeting. She stays with that Hard Question until she is able to report a victory or praise.

Try not to work on too many areas at one time. Instead, the group may want to focus on the one most in need of attention. Another reasonable goal is to commit to make one change, to correct a weakness reflected by a Hard Question.

Since we cannot discern the heart or motive of another, one member should never attempt to select a Hard Question for another. Remember, accountability is voluntary yielding. Most women in my pilot group agreed that the Hard Questions challenged them and made them more aware of their desired personal goal.

Here are some questions that can help your Heart Friends grow in Christlikeness. Regardless of the questions you choose or the group chooses, the last question should be, "Have you been truthful in all your answers?"

1. Do you spend time alone with God on a regular basis?
2. Have you compromised your integrity in any way?
3. In general, is your thought life pure?
4. Do you spend time daily in prayer?
5. Do you pray for others in this group?
6. In what ways do you demonstrate a servant's heart?
7. Do you give to the Lord's work financially?
8. Do you treat your peers and coworkers as people loved by God?

9. Do you take time to show compassion for others in need?
10. What has God told you to do that you are not doing?
11. Since we last met, in what way(s) have you stepped out in faith?
12. Since we last met, in what way(s) have you shrunk back in fear or disbelief?
13. As a pattern, do you find yourself forsaking gathering for worship with other believers?
14. Since we last met, have you shared your faith with anyone?
15. What have you done for someone that led to his or her edification?
16. Are the "visible" you and the "real" you consistent?
17. Is your speech generally full of flattery?
18. Do you ever expose yourself to any explicit materials that would not glorify God?
19. Do you exercise and otherwise take care of your physical body?
20. Have you ever shared the gospel with an unbeliever?
21. Do you eat properly, monitor your intake of sweets, and drink plenty of water?
22. Are you faithful to get the necessary amount of rest and sleep?
23. Do you tend to allow a person or a circumstance to rob you of your joy?
24. Are you a testimony to the greatness of Jesus Christ?
25. Do you allow your mind to entertain inappropriate sexual thoughts?
26. Have you ever hurt another person by your words—shared either face-to-face or behind his or her back?
27. Have you succumbed to any addictive behavior?
28. Do you harbor resentment or anger toward another person?
29. Are there times you allow envy or jealousy to come into your heart?
30. Do you ever secretly wish for someone else's misfortune so that you might excel or be elevated?
31. Are you completely above reproach in your financial dealings?
32. Do you spend quality time with your family?
33. Do you spend time cultivating friendships?
34. Do you tell half-truths, outright lies, or exaggerations to impress others or to place yourself in a favorable light?
35. Are you on time for meetings?
36. Are you an encourager to your family?
37. Have you removed anything from your procrastination list?
38. Did you do something this week that made you laugh?

SOUL CARE VERSUS SERVING OTHERS
A Balance Checklist

We were created for balance, and feel the difference in our souls when our lives tilt too far in one direction. Often we feel we must take on either the service life of Martha or the devoted life of Mary (see Luke 10:38-42). It is, however, not a matter of either, but of both. In her book *Having a Mary Heart in a Martha World*, Joanna Weaver suggests some "signs" that we may need to give attention to one or the other.

Signs You May Need More Time Serving Others

* *Slight depression.* You feel a vague unhappiness, a sense of being down.
* *Resentful of intrusions.* Rather than welcoming people into your life, you find yourself wishing they would go away.
* *Frustrated over life's direction.* You feel a sense of purposelessness and sometimes wonder, *Is this all there is?*
* *Increasingly self-indulgent.* You feel an itch to treat yourself with favorite foods or shopping.
* *Apathetic attitude.* Very little moves you. You know your compassion level is low, but part of you doesn't care.
* *Low energy level.* Like the Dead Sea, you may have many inlets, but no outlets; therefore, you are growing stagnant.

Signs You May Need More Personal Soul Care

* *Irritability and frustration.* Defensive and about to snap, you are especially short-tempered with those you perceive as lazy or uncooperative.
* *Uncomfortable with quiet.* Silence makes you nervous, so you're quick to turn on the TV or the radio.
* *Low joy threshold.* It has been a long time since you've sensed that undercurrent of joy and abundance running through your heart.
* *Sense of isolation.* You feel all alone; no one is there for you and no one understands.
* *Compulsion to do more.* You are haunted by a sense that you must do more and more, even though you know your plate is full.
* *Sense of dryness and emptiness.* No wonder! You have many outlets and demands, but no inlets or source of strength.[14]

TIPS FOR TACKLING TIME

Managing time is a lifelong process, not a one-time goal to be achieved. We all have the same 24 hours in a day, and we all have a choice as to how we will use many of these hours. There are two extremes in managing time: compulsively organized and comfortably cluttered.

I (Margaret) cringe when someone says, "Well, you are always so busy." I prefer to hear someone describe my life as, "full of purpose and meaning." What about you?

May this be said of me and of you:

> Here lies a woman who was always busy.
> She managed her schedule without getting dizzy.
> She put her Lord first and He kept her in line —
> While managing her life, one day at a time.

Fourteen Time-Saving Tips

1. **Start each day with a quiet time.** Most of us are in a hurry, but neglecting our relationship with God will cause us to forfeit His guidance.

2. **Plan and prioritize in writing.** Studies have shown that the success rate for people who write down their goals is significantly higher, perhaps as high as 90 percent, as compared to those who do not.

3. **Be realistic about what you can do.** Block out the amount of time you estimate it will take to complete each task. The best way to accomplish a major goal is to break it into smaller pieces.

4. **Strive for effectiveness over efficiency.** Efficiency is doing the job right. Effectiveness is doing the right job right. Avoid letting routine tasks and work assignments expand beyond reasonable limits.

5. **Eliminate time wasters by first identifying them.** Identify your time wasters, and take the necessary steps to eliminate them.
   - *Telephone Interruptions:* One solution is to use an answering machine and then to block out time to return calls.
   - *Unscheduled Meetings:* Sometimes the failure of other people to manage their time becomes your problem.
   - *Cluttered Desks:* Consider guidelines in Tip no. 10 to destroy the paper monster.
   - *Inability to Say No:* Give yourself some time to consider and pray about a new commitment.
   - *Lack of Clear Communication:* Seek clarification about a task.

6. **Consider your biological prime time.** Are you at your best—your most alert and active—in the early hours or the late hours? Are you a lark or an owl? Identify your energy level, and schedule your most dreaded tasks first. Save no-brainers for the time you are least able to concentrate.

7. **Learn to say no.** This could be one of the hardest lessons to learn. Try responding to a new opportunity by saying, "I will pray about it and get back to you." This allows you time to seek God's will and also to evaluate your priorities and commitment before making a decision.

8. **Create space for the new.** When we get rid of clutter in our overstuffed closets, we usually are amazed at how much space we actually have. The same is true of our time. To find time for something new, we have to reduce or eliminate some old things. For example, if you want to find time to begin an exercise program, looking at your schedule and attempting to fit it in will not work; you must create space for it.

9. **Learn to delegate.** This takes a little longer on the front end but it pays off later. Establishing a team to accomplish tasks at hand will benefit everyone.

10. **Use time-saving systems.** Make sure your new and improved electronic calendar does not cost you time and money. Technology can be a time waster.

11. **Determine to destroy the paper monster.** We never use 80 percent of the paper we keep. Consider these five categories for sorting paper:
    - *To Do Later:* Use this category for shower and wedding invitations, as well as other social events that require a response.
    - *To Pay:* Designate a bill basket.

    ✵ *To File:* Immediately place these items in a folder, and avoid letting things stack up.

    ✵ *To Read:* Keep reading material handy so that you can take advantage of those small segments of time.

    ✵ *To Toss:* Keep a garbage can handy and use it.

12. **Establish a place for everything.** Clutter creates chaos, so determine to de-clutter your home. Ask yourself, *Have I used this in the past six months? Would I pay to have it moved?*

13. **Do not discount small fragments of time.** Try to accomplish several goals at once by combining activities. For example, if you commute, listen to teaching tapes. Keep a book in the car for those times when you get stuck in doctor office waiting rooms.

14. **Remember to assess often and adjust where needed.** Learning to make an honest assessment of daily activities will help you reclaim those extra minutes we all desire. After all, we all want our lives to count for eternity.

"See then that ye walk circumspectly, not as fools, but as wise. Redeeming the time, because the days are evil. Wherefore be ye not unwise, but understanding what the will of the Lord is" (Eph.5:15-17, KJV).

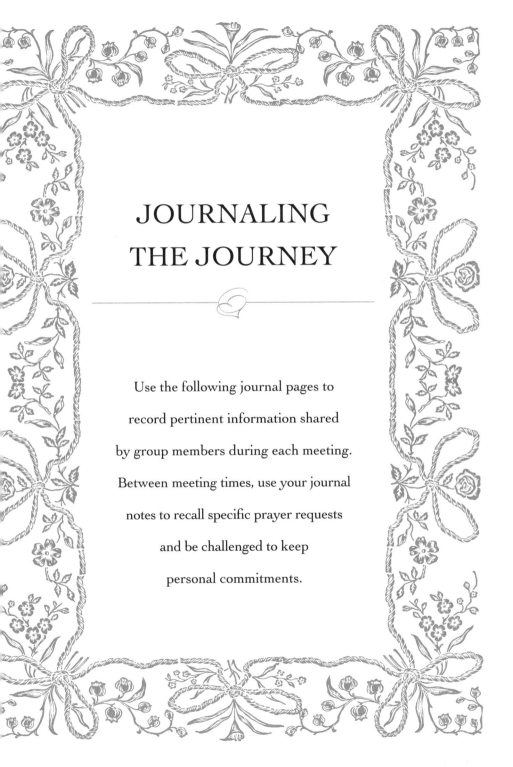

JOURNALING
THE JOURNEY

Use the following journal pages to
record pertinent information shared
by group members during each meeting.
Between meeting times, use your journal
notes to recall specific prayer requests
and be challenged to keep
personal commitments.

HEART FRIENDS

1
WEEK

"For His divine power has given us everything required for life and godliness, through the knowledge of Him who called us by His own glory and goodness." —2 Peter 1:3

MEETING DATE

FACILITATOR

NEXT MEETING DATE

MY HARD QUESTION

PRAYER REQUESTS:

"TALK IT THROUGH" REFLECTIONS:

CUSTOMIZED COMMITMENTS:

"Now may the God of peace Himself sanctify you completely. And may your spirit, soul, and body be kept sound and blameless for the coming of our Lord Jesus Christ."
—1 Thessalonians 5:23

WEEK 2

MY HARD QUESTION:

MEETING DATE

FACILITATOR

NEXT MEETING DATE

PRAYER REQUESTS:

"TALK IT THROUGH" REFLECTIONS:

CUSTOMIZED COMMITMENTS:

3

WEEK

"Set your minds on what is above, not what is on the earth." —Colossians 3:2

MEETING DATE

FACILITATOR

NEXT MEETING DATE

MY HARD QUESTION

PRAYER REQUESTS:

"TALK IT THROUGH" REFLECTIONS:

CUSTOMIZED COMMITMENTS:

"Devote yourselves to prayer; stay alert in it with thanksgiving." —Colossians 3:2

WEEK 4

MY HARD QUESTION:

MEETING DATE

FACILITATOR

NEXT MEETING DATE

PRAYER REQUESTS:

"TALK IT THROUGH" REFLECTIONS:

CUSTOMIZED COMMITMENTS:

HEART &FRIENDS

5 WEEK

"Dear friends, if God loved us in this way, we also must love one another."
—1 John 4:11

MEETING DATE

FACILITATOR

NEXT MEETING DATE

MY HARD QUESTION

PRAYER REQUESTS:

"TALK IT THROUGH" REFLECTIONS:

CUSTOMIZED COMMITMENTS:

"Pray constantly. Give thanks in everything, for this is God's will for you in Christ Jesus." —1 Thessalonians 5:17-18

WEEK 6

MY HARD QUESTION:

MEETING DATE

FACILITATOR

NEXT MEETING DATE

PRAYER REQUESTS:

"TALK IT THROUGH" REFLECTIONS:

CUSTOMIZED COMMITMENTS:

7

WEEK

"Love the Lord your God with all your heart, with all your soul, with all your mind, and with all your strength." — Mark 12:30

MEETING DATE

FACILITATOR

NEXT MEETING DATE

MY HARD QUESTION

PRAYER REQUESTS:

"TALK IT THROUGH" REFLECTIONS:

CUSTOMIZED COMMITMENTS:

"I am the vine; you are the branches. The one who remains in Me and I in Him produces much fruit, because you can do nothing without Me." — John 15:5

WEEK 8

MY HARD QUESTION: _____

_____

_____

_____

MEETING DATE
_____

FACILITATOR
_____

NEXT MEETING DATE
_____

PRAYER REQUESTS: _____

_____

_____

_____

_____

_____

_____

_____

_____

_____

_____

"TALK IT THROUGH" REFLECTIONS:

_____

_____

_____

_____

_____

_____

CUSTOMIZED COMMITMENTS:

_____

_____

_____

_____

_____

_____

_____

9

WEEK

"Therefore, submit to God. But resist the Devil, and he will flee from you.
Draw near to God, and He will draw near to you." —James 4:7-8

MEETING DATE

FACILITATOR

NEXT MEETING DATE

MY HARD QUESTION

PRAYER REQUESTS:

"TALK IT THROUGH" REFLECTIONS:

CUSTOMIZED COMMITMENTS:

"Jesus said to them again, 'Peace to you! As the Father has sent Me, I also send you.'"
—John 20:21

WEEK 10

MY HARD QUESTION:
_____
_____
_____

MEETING DATE
_____

FACILITATOR
_____

NEXT MEETING DATE
_____

PRAYER REQUESTS:
_____
_____
_____
_____
_____
_____
_____
_____
_____
_____

"TALK IT THROUGH" REFLECTIONS:
_____
_____
_____
_____
_____
_____
_____

CUSTOMIZED COMMITMENTS:
_____
_____
_____
_____
_____
_____
_____
_____

HEART❤️FRIENDS

11 WEEK

"But you will receive power when the Holy Spirit has come upon you, and you will be
My witnesses in Jerusalem, in all Judea and Samaria, and to the ends of the earth."
—Acts 1:8

MEETING DATE

FACILITATOR

NEXT MEETING DATE

MY HARD QUESTION

PRAYER REQUESTS:

"TALK IT THROUGH" REFLECTIONS:

CUSTOMIZED COMMITMENTS:

"For I am not ashamed of the gospel, because it is God's power for salvation to everyone who believes, first to the Jew, and also to the Greek." —Romans 1:16

WEEK 12

MY HARD QUESTION:

MEETING DATE

FACILITATOR

NEXT MEETING DATE

PRAYER REQUESTS:

"TALK IT THROUGH" REFLECTIONS:

CUSTOMIZED COMMITMENTS:

13

WEEK

"For from Him and through Him and to Him are all things.
To Him be the glory forever. Amen." —Romans 11:36

MY HARD QUESTION

MEETING DATE

FACILITATOR

NEXT MEETING DATE

PRAYER REQUESTS:

"TALK IT THROUGH" REFLECTIONS:

CUSTOMIZED COMMITMENTS:

"No one lights a lamp and puts it in the cellar or under a basket, but on a lampstand, so that those who come in may see its light." —Luke 11:33

WEEK 14

MY HARD QUESTION: _____

MEETING DATE

FACILITATOR

NEXT MEETING DATE

PRAYER REQUESTS:

"TALK IT THROUGH" REFLECTIONS:

CUSTOMIZED COMMITMENTS:

15

WEEK

"So we do not focus on what is seen, but on what is unseen; for what is seen is temporary, but what is unseen is eternal." —2 Corinthians 4:18

MEETING DATE

FACILITATOR

NEXT MEETING DATE

MY HARD QUESTION

PRAYER REQUESTS:

"TALK IT THROUGH" REFLECTIONS:

CUSTOMIZED COMMITMENTS:

"Whoever is faithful in very little is also faithful in much, and whoever is unrighteous in very little is also unrighteous in much."—Luke 16:10

WEEK 16

MY HARD QUESTION: _____

_____

_____

MEETING DATE

FACILITATOR

NEXT MEETING DATE

PRAYER REQUESTS: _____

"TALK IT THROUGH" REFLECTIONS:

CUSTOMIZED COMMITMENTS:

HEART✥FRIENDS

17 WEEK

"Each person should do as he has decided in his heart—not out of regret or out of necessity, for God loves a cheerful giver."—2 Corinthians 9:7

MEETING DATE

FACILITATOR

NEXT MEETING DATE

MY HARD QUESTION

PRAYER REQUESTS:

"TALK IT THROUGH" REFLECTIONS:

CUSTOMIZED COMMITMENTS:

"From Him the whole body, fitted and knit together by every supporting ligament, promotes the growth of the body for building up itself in love by the proper working of each individual part."—Ephesians 4:16

WEEK 18

MY HARD QUESTION:

_____

_____

_____

MEETING DATE

_____

FACILITATOR

_____

NEXT MEETING DATE

PRAYER REQUESTS:

_____

_____

_____

_____

_____

_____

_____

_____

_____

_____

_____

_____

"TALK IT THROUGH" REFLECTIONS:

_____

_____

_____

_____

_____

_____

CUSTOMIZED COMMITMENTS:

_____

_____

_____

_____

_____

_____

_____

_____

19 WEEK

"But the fruit of the Spirit is love, joy, peace, patience, kindness, goodness, faith, gentleness, self-control. Against such things there is no law." —Galatians 5:22-23

MEETING DATE

FACILITATOR

NEXT MEETING DATE

MY HARD QUESTION

PRAYER REQUESTS:

"TALK IT THROUGH" REFLECTIONS:

CUSTOMIZED COMMITMENTS:

"I am sure of this, that He who started a good work in you will carry it on to completion until the day of Christ Jesus."—Philippians 1:6

WEEK

20

MY HARD QUESTION: _____

MEETING DATE

_____

_____

FACILITATOR

NEXT MEETING DATE

PRAYER REQUESTS: _____

"TALK IT THROUGH" REFLECTIONS:

CUSTOMIZED COMMITMENTS:

21
WEEK

"But have nothing to do with irreverent and silly myths. Rather, train yourself in godliness." — 1 Timothy 4:7

MEETING DATE

FACILITATOR

NEXT MEETING DATE

MY HARD QUESTION

PRAYER REQUESTS:

"TALK IT THROUGH" REFLECTIONS:

CUSTOMIZED COMMITMENTS:

"He predestined us to be adopted through Jesus Christ for Himself, according to His favor and will." — Ephesians 1:5

WEEK **22**

MY HARD QUESTION:

MEETING DATE

FACILITATOR

NEXT MEETING DATE

PRAYER REQUESTS:

"TALK IT THROUGH" REFLECTIONS:

CUSTOMIZED COMMITMENTS:

23 WEEK

"And my God will supply all your needs according to His riches in glory in Christ Jesus." — Philippians 4:19

MEETING DATE

FACILITATOR

NEXT MEETING DATE

MY HARD QUESTION

PRAYER REQUESTS:

"TALK IT THROUGH" REFLECTIONS:

CUSTOMIZED COMMITMENTS:

"So don't throw away your confidence, which has a great reward. For you need endurance, so that after you have done God's will, you may receive what was promised." —Hebrews 10:35-36

MY HARD QUESTION:

_____

_____

_____

MEETING DATE

_____

FACILITATOR

_____

NEXT MEETING DATE

_____

PRAYER REQUESTS:

_____

_____

_____

_____

_____

_____

_____

_____

_____

_____

"TALK IT THROUGH" REFLECTIONS:

_____

_____

_____

_____

_____

_____

CUSTOMIZED COMMITMENTS:

_____

_____

_____

_____

_____

_____

_____

25 WEEK

"Now may the God of hope fill you with all joy and peace in believing, so that you may overflow with hope by the power of the Holy Spirit." — Romans 15:13

MEETING DATE

FACILITATOR

NEXT MEETING DATE

MY HARD QUESTION

PRAYER REQUESTS:

"TALK IT THROUGH" REFLECTIONS:

CUSTOMIZED COMMITMENTS:

"When the Messiah, who is your life, is revealed, then you also will be revealed with Him in glory." —Colossians 3:4

WEEK 26

MY HARD QUESTION:
_____
_____
_____

MEETING DATE
_____

FACILITATOR
_____

NEXT MEETING DATE
_____

PRAYER REQUESTS:
_____
_____
_____
_____
_____
_____
_____
_____
_____
_____
_____

"TALK IT THROUGH" REFLECTIONS:
_____
_____
_____
_____
_____
_____
_____
_____

CUSTOMIZED COMMITMENTS:
_____
_____
_____
_____
_____
_____
_____
_____

27 WEEK

"So because of Christ, I am pleased in weaknesses, in insults, in catastrophes, in persecutions, and in pressures. For when I am weak, then I am strong."

—2 Corinthians 12:10

MEETING DATE

FACILITATOR

NEXT MEETING DATE

MY HARD QUESTION

PRAYER REQUESTS:

"TALK IT THROUGH" REFLECTIONS:

CUSTOMIZED COMMITMENTS:

"The Lord answered her, 'Martha, Martha, you are worried and upset about many things, but one thing is necessary. Mary has made the right choice, and it will not be taken away from her.' " —Luke 10:41-42

WEEK 28

MY HARD QUESTION:

_____

_____

_____

MEETING DATE

_____

FACILITATOR

_____

NEXT MEETING DATE

_____

PRAYER REQUESTS:

_____

_____

_____

_____

_____

_____

_____

_____

_____

_____

"TALK IT THROUGH" REFLECTIONS:

_____

_____

_____

_____

_____

_____

CUSTOMIZED COMMITMENTS:

_____

_____

_____

_____

_____

_____

_____

29 WEEK

"Rejoice in the Lord always. I will say it again: Rejoice!" — Philippians 4:4

MY HARD QUESTION

MEETING DATE

FACILITATOR

NEXT MEETING DATE

PRAYER REQUESTS:

"TALK IT THROUGH" REFLECTIONS:

CUSTOMIZED COMMITMENTS:

*"But, as the One who called you is holy, you also are to be holy in all your conduct; for it is written, **Be holy, because I am holy.**"*—1 Peter 1:15-16

WEEK 30

MY HARD QUESTION: _____

_____

_____

_____

MEETING DATE

_____

FACILITATOR

_____

NEXT MEETING DATE

PRAYER REQUESTS: _____

_____

_____

_____

_____

_____

_____

_____

_____

_____

_____

"TALK IT THROUGH" REFLECTIONS: _____

_____

_____

_____

_____

_____

_____

_____

CUSTOMIZED COMMITMENTS: _____

_____

_____

_____

_____

_____

_____

_____

ENDNOTES

1. James Strong, *The New Strong's Exhaustive Concordance of the Bible: Hebrew and Chaldee Dictionary* (Nashville: TN: Thomas Nelson, 1990), 58.
2. Spiros Zodhiates et al., eds., *The Complete Word Study Dictionary: New Testament, Rev. Ed.* (Chattanooga, TN: AMG Publishers, 1993), 819.
3. Zodhiates, *Complete Word Study Dictionary*, 125.
4. Ibid., 1107.
5. A wife and mother of three girls, Candace enjoys sharing the truths of God's Word with women and writing poems that touch the heart. It is her "joy to be a blessing" to others through poems such as "Hide and Seek." She considers Margaret Kennedy a dear Heart Friend.
6. Zodhiates, *Complete Word Study Dictionary*, 1427.
7. Ibid., 873.
8. "James A. Garfield Quotes," BrainyQuote, *http.//www.brainyquote.com* (accessed February 24, 2005).
9. Lee Ezell, "The Paint Brush," from the book *Will the Real Me Please Stand Up?* Used by permission of Ezell Communications.
10. Zodhiates, *Complete Word Study Dictionary*, 597.
11. Beth Moore, *When Godly People Do Ungodly Things: Video* (Nashville, TN: LifeWay Press, 2003), group session 4.
12. Strong, *Strong's Exhaustive Concordance: Greek Testament*, 70.
13. Ibid., 75.
14. Reprinted from *Having a Mary Heart in a Martha World* Copyright © 2002 by Joanna Weaver, Waterbrook Press, Colorado Springs, CO. All rights reserved.
15. D. Edmond Hiebert, *1 Peter* (Chicago, IL: Moody Press, 1992), 113.
16. Warren W. Wiersbe, comp. *The Best of A. W. Tozer* (Camp Hill, PA: Christian Publications, 1979), 112-114.

EVALUATING HEALTH AND EFFECTIVENESS
Measuring your group's growth, progress, and direction

Based on your perception of your group, rate each item using a range of 1 *(Never)* to 7 *(Always)*. For example, a satisfactory ("Sometimes") rating might be a 3 or a 4. In the blank beside each question, place the number that best indicates your group's progress.

Complete this evaluation every three months. Make adjustments to your training or accountability groups as needed.

_____ 1. Do we begin and end our meetings on time?

_____ 2. Do we open and close our meetings with prayer?

_____ 3. Are we consistently sharing the responsibility of facilitating the group?

_____ 4. Are we monitoring our individual sharing and discussion time?

_____ 5. Does the group provide a nurturing atmosphere?

_____ 6. Are we practicing sensitivity in listening?

_____ 7. Are members exhibiting transparency?

_____ 8. Are we faithfully praying for each other between meetings?

_____ 9. Is this group helping me maintain God's standard of holiness in my life?

_____ 10. Are we reaching our personal goals?

_____ 11. Are we guarding our conversation?

_____ 12. Is this group equipping me to live a well-ordered and balanced life?

_____ 13. Are group members living in a way that make the gospel attractive to unbelievers?

_____ 14. Does my group promote the daily Christian disciplines of prayer and Bible study?

_____ 15. Are we becoming tempered Christians, walking by faith, demonstrating hope, and manifesting true biblical love in all of our relationships?

Indicate here any comments on specific questions.

_____

_____

_____

_____

_____

_____

_____

FOR ALL HEART FRIENDS

It is our prayer that by the time you read this page, you will find yourself ready to be part of an accountability group. As you can tell, our groups have been a source of real encouragement to us.

The Apostle Paul knew we would need encouragement as we live out our calling (see 1 Thess. 5:11). An accountability group should be a place where you give and receive encouragement.

Peter was on target when he told us to *"love one another deeply, from the heart"* (1 Pet. 1:22, NIV). Of what kind of love was Peter speaking? It is a love of rational good will that desires the highest good for the one loved, even at the expense of self.[15]

What an awesome experience to be loved in this way! Can it be true? Oh, yes! I have seen and experienced such love and acceptance from my Heart Friends, and this kind of relationship can be yours.

Enlightenment comes from the Holy Spirit, and God's Spirit is invited into a place where there is unity. Inspired by encouragers, unity grows out of the concern your group members express for one another. How does this take place in the context of an accountability group? Read Acts 4:31 to find out.

We want to leave you with insights from A.W. Tozer:

> "True spirituality manifests itself in certain dominate *desires*. These are ever-present, deep-settled wants sufficiently powerful to motivate and control the life."
> 1. To be holy rather than happy
> 2. To see the honor of God advanced through his life even if he himself must suffer temporary dishonor or loss
> 3. To carry his cross when voluntarily in obedience
> 4. The desire to see things from God's perspective
> 5. The desire to die right rather that live wrong
> 6. The desire to see others advance at his expense
> 7. The desire to be useful rather than famous
> "All this," Tozer explains, "must be the operation of the Holy Spirit. …No man can become spiritual by himself."[16]

Reflect and be blessed, for the kingdom's sake,

Margaret and Shirley

PREPARATION AND PROMOTION

Our goal in developing this workbook-journal is to provide you, individually or corporately as a body of believers, the benefits of beginning and maintaining a small accountability group. Our desire is to put into your hands a tool that will assist you in living a life of accountability, reaching your maximum potential for the glory of God, and maintaining His standard of godliness in your personal walk.

PERSONAL PREPARATION

If you are your church's women's ministry leader, request a meeting with the staff member who overseas women's ministry. By all means, solicit his or her support before beginning an accountability program. If no staff member is assigned, then set up an appointment with your pastor to seek his support before continuing. Be prepared to receive and respond to any input, questions, and concerns.

PUBLICITY PREPARATION

Here are some suggestions for publicizing the opportunities *Heart Friends* provides.
- Mail women an attractive flyer that highlights the date and time of the kickoff session.
- If your church has an automated phone messaging system, select a woman with an energetic voice to record a message for the women of your church.
- Place posters throughout your church buildings.
- Promote the opening session at an already scheduled women's event.
- Make an announcement in Adult Sunday School classes.
- Be enthusiastic! Nothing is as effective and influential as personal enthusiasm. Enlist interested women to talk it up among their peers.

INTENTIONAL PREPARATION

This ministry is designed for churches of all sizes. Training is formatted for four weeks, with each session requiring approximately one hour. Margaret's leader guide procedures for each session may be found on pages 123-126.

Each week women come together for a time of teaching and sharing as they learn accountability principles. At the end of the four-week period, each member will have completed the "Getting Started" section of *Heart Friends* and answered the questions posed. The hope is that, by the end of this four-week training, small accountability groups will develop.

If your total attendance is ten or less, you may want to maintain one group. With ten or more women attending, divide them into equal subgroups. The group leader enlists a facilitator for each subgroup. Each week women are assigned to a new group, which increases opportunities for potential accountability friends. The group leader is responsible for group rotation.

Each woman will need her own copy of *Heart Friends*. Journals should be made available at the kickoff session. Members should agree to attend all four sessions and complete assigned readings. Each woman should bring her Bible each week.

PRAYER PREPARATION

- Pray, asking God to reveal His will and timing for introducing the concept of accountability groups in your church.
- Listen to the women around you as they engage in daily conversation.
- Observe women in Bible study as they express their needs.
- Ask God to help you discern the cry of their hearts.

Margaret: In recent year, as I have traveled throughout the country teaching and training women, I have detected heightened interest whenever the word *account-ability* is mentioned. I began to sense that this was God at work.

I began to pray for God's timing in my own church. I discussed briefly the possibility of presenting accountability groups to our Women's Ministry leader. She began to pray and wait as well.

As I led a group of women of various ages through a Bible study, an opportunity arose to poll them: "How many of you would be interested in coming together for a few weeks to learn the benefits of accountability and how to get started?" Nearly every hand shot up and I heard, "When can we start?"

Women had already begun asking our Women's Ministry leader to begin this training. We discerned this to be God working and extending an invitation to us to join Him in that work. We continued to pray, seeking the input and approval of appropriate staff members. We talked about using this workbook-journal in a trial session with a small group of women, before opening it to the entire church. We spent time brainstorming how accountability groups might work in our church and left excited about what God was going to do in our midst.

Prayer preparation must precede any other preparation. Waiting for God's timing is of the utmost importance.

Select a date, time, and place to hold an informal fellowship for all women interested in learning about a life of accountability. During this kickoff session, all women will remain in one large group.

1. Serve soft drinks and light refreshments. Welcome everyone and provide name tags.

2. Begin with a short get-acquainted icebreaker. *(Jump Starts and Soft Landings* or *Ice-Breakers and Heart-Warmers* [Serendipty House®] are excellent resources and are available through LifeWay Christian Stores.).

3. *(Group leader)* Open in prayer. Having reviewed *Heart Friends* in advance, give a short presentation of the importance of living the accountable life.

4. If some women attending are currently involved in an accountability group, ask them to share benefits they have received. If not, enlist someone to share her desire for accountability and how she expects to benefit from being in a small group.

5. Distribute a *Heart Friends* journal to each participant. If women are purchasing their copies, receive their money now. Point out the various features of *Heart Friends* based on the information in "Using *Heart Friends*" (pp. 6-7). Before the next meeting, ask women to study and do assigned activities on the following content:
  ⊛ Accountability Understood (pp. 9-13)
  ⊛ Accountable to One Another (pp. 14-16)
  ⊛ Accountability Advantages (pp. 17-20)

6. Direct women to the section entitled "Asking the Hard Questions" (pp. 81-82). Instruct them to select one question from this list for which to be held accountable by another group member. Ask each woman to turn to the woman on her right. Each should share the question she chose and give her new Heart Friend permission to hold her accountable for this work until the next meeting. Each woman should agree to (1) pray for each other and her area of concern and (2) make at least one contact during the coming week.

7. Close in prayer and encourage women to return next week. Based on the anticipated attendance, locate any additional rooms that may be needed for small groups during Sessions 2-4.

2

1. *(Group leader and facilitators)* Greet ladies as they arrive, and thank them for returning. Introduce newcomers and give them name tags. Encourage everyone to enjoy the refreshments.

2. *(Group leader)* If the size of your group calls for it, assign women to predetermined small groups. Vary groups and facilitators each week. If your initial group is less than or close to ten, keep everyone together for the following activities.

3. Encourage women to make contact with this week's Heart Friend and to ask each other the Hard Question. After opening the total group in prayer, share the poem "Hide and Seek" (p. 13). Comment as follows: *It is not in our human nature to seek accountability. We should recognize our accountablity to God before we can consider becoming accountable to other believers.* Dismiss women into small groups, if appropriate.

4. *(Small-group facilitator)* Lead in discussing this content from *Heart Friends*, and answer questions that may have surfaced:
   ❀ Accountability Understood (pp. 9-13)
   ❀ Accountable to One Another (pp. 14-16)
   ❀ Accountability Advantages (pp. 17-20).
   If time allows, spend the last ten minutes discussing a Conversation Guide of your choice in this journal.

5. Encourage women to continue working through their *Heart Friends* journal. Ask them to complete, for next week's discussion, assigned activities for these topics:
   ❀ Attributes of an Accountable Person (pp. 21-23)
   ❀ Acquiring an Accountability Group (pp. 24-25).

   Direct women to turn to the section entitled "Asking the Hard Questions" (pp. 81-82). Instruct them to select one question for which to be held accountable. They may repeat the previous Hard Question.
   At this time, each woman should turn to the woman on her right and share her Hard Question. She will give her new Heart Friend permission to hold her accountable for this work until the next meeting. Each woman should agree to pray for each other in these areas of growth and to make at least one contact during the week.

6. Conclude in prayer.

SESSION 3

1. *(Group leader and facilitators)* Welcome women and encourage them to enjoy refreshments and fellowship.

2. *(Group leader)* Remind ladies to locate their Heart Friend and to ask each other their Hard Question. Open the total group in prayer.

3. *(Small-group faclitator,)* After a creative reading of "The Paint Brush" (p. 32), lead a discussion of the following content:
   - Attributes of an Accountable Person (pp. 21-23)
   - Acquiring an Accountability Group (pp. 24-25).

4. If time permits, spend the last ten minutes of the meeting discussing a Conversation Guide of your choice. Indicate how Conversation Guides are an important tool for use in accountability groups.

5. Encourage women to continue working through their *Heart Friends* journal. Assign this content for next week's discussion:
   - Accountability Action Plan (pp. 26-27)
   - Suggested Meeting Format and Activities (pp. 28-29)
   - Additional Accountability Questions (pp. 30-31)

6. Direct women to the section entitled "Asking the Hard Questions" (pp. 81-82). Instruct them to select one Hard Question for which to be held accountable. They may wish to use a previously selected Hard Question.

   At this time, ask each woman to turn to the woman on her right and to share her Hard Question. In so doing, she is giving her Heart Friend permission to hold her accountable for this work.

   Each woman should agree to pray for the other in her area of accountability and to make at least one contact during the week.

7. Dismiss in prayer.

4 SESSION

1. *(Group leader and small-group facilitators)* Greet the woman as they arrive. Thank them for attending this training. Consider scheduling additional time for fellowship or refreshments, to make your closing session special.

2. As the women arrive, encourage them to make contact with this week's Heart Friend and to ask each other their Hard Question.

3. After opening in prayer, dismiss women into small groups.

4. *(Small-group facilitator)* Discuss the following content from *Heart Friends*:
   - Accountability Action Plan (pp. 26-27)
   - Suggested Meeting Format and Activities (pp. 28-29)
   - Additional Accountability Questions (pp. 30-31)

5. If time permits, spend the last ten minutes discussing one of the Conversation Guides in this journal. Ask women to share how they have benefitted from using Conversation Guides, and highlight their use in future small groups.

6. Encourage women by reminding them that they are now equipped to find an acccountability partner as God leads. This partner may or may not be a part of this particular training group.

7. Direct women to read "Setting Personal Goals" and to begin the process of using the "Personal Goal Worksheet" in *Heart Friends* (pp. 34-38). Encourage them also to share their story using "My Personal Testimony" on page 39.

8. Schedule a time for celebration and testimonies that includes all participants. Close in prayer.

9. If members qualify for Christian Growth Study Plan credit (see p. 128), gather forms now.

Use this format to offer accountability group training on a semiannual or annual basis. Evaluate training and make adjustments as needed.

HOW TO BECOME A CHRISTIAN

By nature, your heart turns from God and rebels against Him. The Bible calls this "sin." Romans 3:23 tells us, *"For all have sinned and fall short of the glory of God."*

Yet God loves you and wants to save you from sin, to offer you a new life of hope. One verse Heart Friends have focused on is John 10:10; it tell us, *"I* (meaning Jesus) *have come that they may have life and have it in abundance."*

To give you this gift of salvation, God made a way through His Son, Jesus Christ. Romans 5:8 explains: *"But God proves His own love for us in that while we were still sinners Christ died for us!"*

You receive this gift by faith alone according to Ephesians 2:8-9: *"For by grace you are saved through faith, and this is not from yourselves; it is God's gift — not from works, so that no one can boast."*

Faith is a decision of your heart demonstrated by genuine repentance and changed actions in your life. Romans 10:9 says, *"If you confess with your mouth 'Jesus is Lord,' and believe in your heart that God raaised Him from the dead, you will be saved."*

If you are choosing right now to believe Jesus died for your sins and to receive new life through Him, pray a prayer similar to the following, in which you accept what He has done for you and thank Him for your new life.

> Dear God, I know I am a sinner. I believe Jesus died to forgive me of my sins. I now accept Your offer of eternal life. Thank You for forgiving me of all my sin. Thank You for my new life. From this day forward, I will choose to follow You.

If this expresses the prayer of your heart, we want to help you grow as a new Christian. Tell your pastor or group leader about your decision.

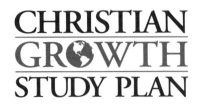

CHRISTIAN GROWTH STUDY PLAN

In the Christian Growth Study Plan this book *Heart Friends: Beginning and Maintaining a Small Accountability Group* is a resource for course credit in the subject area Women's Enrichment of the Christian Growth category of plans. To receive credit, (1) read the book, complete the learning activities, show your work to your women's ministry leader, and participate in an ongoing small group; OR (2) attend the four sessions, complete the learning activities; and participate in an ongoing small group. Complete the following information; this page may be duplicated.

Send the completed page to:
Christian Growth Study Plan, One LifeWay Plaza Nashville, TN 37234-0117; FAX: (615)251-5067; Email: cgspnet@lifeway.com

For information about the Christian Growth Plan, refer to the Christian Growth Study Plan Catalog. It is located online at www.lifeway.com/cg If you do not have access to the Internet, contact th Christian Growth Study Plan office (1.800.968.55) for the specific plan you need for your ministry.

Heart Friends: Beginning and Maintaining a Small Accountability Group
COURSE NUMBER: CG-1126

PARTICIPANT INFORMATION

Social Security Number (USA ONLY-optional)	Personal CGSP Number*	Date of Birth (MONTH, DAY, YEAR)
– –	–	– –

Name (First, Middle, Last)	Home Phone
	– –

Address (Street, Route, or P.O. Box)	City, State, or Province	Zip/Postal Code

Please check appropriate box: ❑ Resource purchased by self ❑ Resource purchased by church ❑ Other

CHURCH INFORMATION

Church Name

Address (Street, Route, or P.O. Box)	City, State, or Province	Zip/Postal Code

CHANGE REQUEST ONLY

☐ Former Name

☐ Former Address	City, State, or Province	Zip/Postal Code

☐ Former Church	City, State, or Province	Zip/Postal Code

Signature of Pastor, Conference Leader, or Other Church Leader	Date

*New participants are requested but not required to give SS# and date of birth. Existing participants, please give CGSP# when using SS# for the first time. Thereafter, only one ID# is required. **Mail to:** Christian Growth Study Plan, One LifeWay Plaza, Nashville, TN 37234-0117. Fax: (615)251-5067.